D1014964

ARAB-AMERICAN AND MUSLIM WRITERS

MULTICULTURAL VOICES

AFRICAN-AMERICAN WRITERS

ARAB-AMERICAN AND MUSLIM WRITERS

ASIAN-AMERICAN WRITERS

HISPANIC-AMERICAN WRITERS

NATIVE AMERICAN WRITERS

MULTICULTURAL VOICES

ARAB-AMERICAN AND MUSLIM WRITERS

REBECCA LAYTON

CHELSEA HOUSE
PUBLISHERS
An imprint of Infobase Publishing

MULTICULTURAL VOICES: Arab-American and Muslim Writers

Copyright © 2010 by Infobase Publishing

Chelsea House
An imprint of Infobase Publishing
132 West 31st Street
New York NY 10001

Library of Congress Cataloging-in-Publication Data
Layton, Rebecca.
    Arab-American and Muslim writers / Rebecca Layton.
        p. cm.—(Multicultural voices)
    Includes bibliographical references and index.
    ISBN 978-1-60413-377-6 (hardcover)
    1. ArabAmericanauthors—Biography—Juvenileliterature. 2. Americanliterature—Arab American authors—History and criticism—Juvenile literature. 3. American literature—Arab American authors—Themes, motives—Juvenile literature. 4. Arab Americans in literature—Juvenile literature. 5. American literature—Muslim authors—History and criticism—Juvenile literature. 6. American literature—Muslim authors—Themes, motives—Juvenile literature. 7. Muslim authors—Biography—Juvenile literature. 8. Muslims in literature—Juvenile literature. I. Title. II. Series.
    PS153.A73L39 2010
    810.9'8927—dc22   2010001365

Chelsea House books are available at special discounts when purchased in bulk quantities for businesses, associations, institutions, or sales promotions. Please call our Special Sales Department in New York at (212) 967-8800 or (800) 322-8755.

You can find Chelsea House on the World Wide Web at
http://www.chelseahouse.com

Series design by Lina Farinella
Cover designed by Alicia Post
Composition by IBT Global, Troy NY
Cover printed by IBT Global, Troy NY
Book printed and bound by IBT Global, Troy NY
Date printed: May 2010
Printed in the United States of America

10 9 8 7 6 5 4 3 2 1

This book is printed on acid-free paper.

All links and Web addresses were checked and verified to be correct at the time of publication. Because of the dynamic nature of the Web, some addresses and links may have changed since publication and may no longer be valid.

CONTENTS

OVERVIEW

WITH ITS DIVERSE PEOPLES, cultures, and religious practices, the Middle East, along with the predominantly Muslim nations of South Asia and northern Africa, has exerted a varied and multifaceted influence on the United States. It is difficult to summarize these contributions, as individuals from a wide range of backgrounds have brought their personal histories, filled with struggle and success, to a new land. Similarly, it is impossible to approach the topic of Arab- and Muslim-American writers with an absolute, all-encompassing statement that would do justice to the rich works and range of themes and concerns they explore. The diverse voices included in this volume do not represent a single vision or share a common set of concerns. The authors do not come from a single place or subscribe to a particular religious or spiritual heritage. Instead, they are writers who have staked out an individual space from which they explore their own relations to identity, culture, religion, and the building or inhabiting of a life in the United States. Some writers, such as Mohja Kahf and Khaled Hosseini, were born into families that immigrated to the United States when they were children. Other authors, such as Claire Messud and Mona Simpson, have a parent who was born outside the United States, but they make no overt association with their Middle Eastern or Muslim heritage. Instead, the individuals included in this survey share perhaps only their diversity and their unique view of and relation to their American-ness. In many of these authors' works, the United States emerges as a powerful, symbolic idea, a place that contains idealized possibilities and grim realities.

The descriptive phrase *Arab American* does not imply a single, unified identity. Arabs are Muslim, Christian, Jewish, or subscribe to no faith at all. Like the Arab-American writers profiled in this volume, these individuals come from vastly different countries and cultures. They may be urban or rural dwellers, religious or secular, modern or traditional. Similarly, Muslim Americans trace their origins to nations in Asia, Africa, and the rest of the inhabited continents. They share only the common thread of immigration, coming to the United States either in the distant or recent past. In addition, there are those Muslims who were born in the United States and have chosen to convert to Islam, often for political reasons. The religion of Islam—and its link to the Arab world—is often misunderstood. As one scholar writes, "Islam plays a fundamental role in Arab America external of the popular notion in the United States that all Arabs are Muslim (or, conversely, that all Muslims are Arab)."

"Black Muslims"

Though the classifications of Arab American and Muslim American as groups have some overlap, they also differ in several key ways. Malcolm X and Amiri Baraka come out of a distinct Muslim-American tradition that is also known as black nationalism, a movement that advocates a black national identity separate from mainstream, white-influenced American culture. Within this tradition of Islam, there are Muslims who have never left the United States and who have chosen to convert at least partly for political reasons. Malcolm X made the argument that the very notion of Western culture, and the Judeo-Christian religious traditions on which it is based, was inherently racist. By becoming *black Muslims* (a term that he did not endorse but that was nonetheless often used to describe his movement), Malcolm felt that African Americans could create their own community based on the self-reliance and autonomy that was necessary to rise above the Christian and Western influences that helped rigidly define American life and identity. He initially was allied with the Nation of Islam, led by the controversial figure Elijah Muhammed, but later broke from the movement and started his own temple. The more that Malcolm X learned about Islam and the more he realized that the American version was a distortion of the faith's inherent teachings, the less extremist he became in his views. The turning point for him was a *hajj*, or pilgrimage, he made to Mecca in 1964, in which he realized that the main truth in Islamic doctrine is that of a universal brotherhood and love.

Fragmented Identities

Despite the variety of cultural and personal positions these writers bring to the page, there are perhaps more similarities among these distinct voices than at first glance. Barbara Nimri Aziz writes in the foreword to the book *Scheherazade's Legacy: Arab and Arab American Women on Writing*, "There are many similarities between Arab and African American experiences in the United States, and Arabs in general would gain much in our struggle for empowerment and recognition by studying our positions vis-à-vis the mainstream white society more closely." She advocates the advice that James Baldwin gave: to write from one's own experience. This freedom to lay claim to one's own experience and to unearth one's own power of testimony and witness is not always or necessarily easy to attain. As Aziz points out, "Arab descendants in America are, to a degree, colonized. Encouraged to forget our beautiful difference, we imbibe so many of the biases and distortions around us. We become ambiguous about our heritage. And a person who is equivocal or confused can never become an artist." Aziz believes it is the job of today's Arab writers to help to rebuild a "fragmented, uncertain identity."

Despite the difficulty that exists in summarizing the work of these writers with one generalized and summative statement, there is nonetheless a distinct Arab-American literary tradition that exists and continues to grow and change in the United States today. Going back to the early years of the twentieth century, an immigrant school of Arabic literature was led by writers from Lebanon and Syria who sought to expand the cultural production of the early generation of Arab Americans and who served as a bridge between East and West. This core group of early Arab-American literati was composed of writers such as Kahlil Gibran (1883–1931), Ameen Rihani (1876–1940), and Mikhail Naimy (1889–1988). They laid the literary groundwork to which subsequent generations have added their voices and visions. In addition, they provided a crucial starting point, a point of departure that initiated the task of reinvention that so often is part of the immigrant experience in the United States. The fact that this first generation of Arab-American writers had newly arrived from their home countries enabled them to cross the bridge from traditional Arabic literary practices and verse forms to embrace a more expanded definition of Arabic literature.

The Personal

In an interview with the *New York Times*, Mohja Kahf addressed the issue of how she writes about the experience of being the "other": "Islam makes you this other race," Kahf told a literature class at Stanford University, noting that the genre should appeal to both American Muslims and outsiders seeking a better understanding of the minority. "I can't not write ethnically, because my characters don't eat pork and they do use incense." Here, Kahf attests to the cultural and religious stereotypes with which Arab- and Muslim-American writers are often saddled. While many of these writers integrate elements of their cultural heritage into their works, they are often burdened with the added task of breaking free of these concerns and labels in an effort to establish their own unique authorial presence.

Writing from one's own personal experience implies a subjectivity and an inward-looking, self-contained focus. The poet Naomi Shihab Nye writes about the small, personal ordinariness involved in the act of writing an essay:

How does it start? Human-sized, with a pocket of tiny mysteries. Turning a word over and over in one's head as hours go by. Finding comfort in the company of a word. . . .

"Why do you write about ordinary things?" people ask and ask again.
Well, what do they have in their lives?
I never understand this question.
You can't miss it.
Well, yes you can.

In one of Nye's works, the ordinary is prominently featured, as a little girl combs her grandmother's hair. Barbara Nimri Aziz responds to the inclusion of this small detail by telling how it affected her: "[Wh]en I read that passage in Nye's story, I was deeply moved, in part because I felt my heritage was retrieved. . . . Perhaps other children comb their grandmothers' hair. Because an Arab woman, Naomi Shihab Nye was the first to articulate it to me, it has greater poignancy. Art, not nostalgia, made the leap." It is the subjective and personal nature of Nye's writing that rang true to Aziz and makes the experience of the "other" one that can be universalized and in which everyone can share.

Politics

Many of the writers in this volume have responded to twenty-first-century political events, most prominent among them the attacks on the World Trade Center on September 11, 2001. Whether explicitly or implicitly, the political environment of a post–September 11 world has influenced writers living in the United States, Arab Americans to a greater extent than others. Arab-American literature scholar Steven Salaita writes, "American society appears somehow to have morphed into a position in which Arab Americans frequently are demonized or mythologized in the service of assorted political strategies." Poet Suheir Hammad brings this point home in a more personal way when she writes in her poem "First Writing Since" of hearing the news of the World Trade Center attacks, "please god, let it be a mistake . . . please don't let it be anyone who looks like my brother . . ." The sense that many Americans hold a stereotyped and racist view of Arabs, Muslims, and Arab Americans makes it all the more necessary to delve into the wide range of contemporary Arab-American writing increasingly featured in the American literary canon today.

One of the overriding themes in all of these works is the problem of finding a home. Even the most so-called assimilated of these authors speaks about the universal search for connection—with family, with country, with themselves. If there is a measure of their sense of belonging, each of these writers could be said to fall somewhere outside this line. Their relative identification—or lack of identification—with their ethnicity or religious heritage is not what is exclusively important; what is crucial is their identification with the human condition and their attempts to present that condition, in all its foibles and delights, to their readers.

KAHLIL GIBRAN

Biography

KAHLIL GIBRAN holds the unique position of being one of the most successful and famous Arab-American writers in the world, as well as one of the most popular authors to write in English. Gibran's work deals mostly with spiritual and visionary themes, specifically using Christian imagery but always with an eye toward universal truths and a mystical view of human love. A poet, artist, and mystic, Kahlil Gibran managed to bridge Eastern and Western philosophy, thought, and religion in his work, transcending cultural differences in pursuit of a message of liberation and higher consciousness. To this day, Gibran remains one of the most widely read authors in English. His masterpiece, *The Prophet,* has been translated into more than 20 languages and was one of the best-selling books of the twentieth century.

Kahlil Gibran was born in 1883 in the town of Bsharri, in Ottoman Syria (present-day northern Lebanon) to a Christian Maronite family; his maternal grandfather was a Maronite priest. Though Gibran did not have any formal early schooling, he was taught Arabic and Syriac by local priests, who also gave him religious training in the Bible. In 1891, when he was 8 years old, his father was sent to prison for tax evasion, and their family home was seized by Ottoman authorities. Gibran's mother, Kamila, moved Kahlil, his older brother, Peter, and two younger sisters, Marianna and Sultana, to live with relatives. Eventually, she decided to take her family to the United States, where her brother had immigrated earlier.

On June 25, 1895, the Gibrans set sail for New York. They settled in Boston's South End, at that time the second-largest Lebanese-Syrian community in the United States. Kahlil's mother found work as a street peddler, selling linens and lace door to door. Kahlil started school that September, in a class designated for immigrants who needed to learn English. He also enrolled in an art school at the local settlement house. His teachers there, impressed with his natural drawing skills, eventually introduced him to the Boston avant-garde artist Fred Holland Day. A photographer and publisher, Day encouraged the young Gibran.

Gibran's mother, concerned that Kahlil was becoming unduly influenced by Western culture, sent him back to Lebanon at the age of 15 to study at a Maronite-run preparatory school in Beirut. After several years of schooling, he returned to Boston in 1902. Shortly before returning, his sister Sultana died of tuberculosis. The following year, Gibran lost his brother to the same disease, and his mother died of cancer. His sister Marianna supported herself and Kahlil with work at a dressmaker's shop.

In 1904, Fred Holland Day hosted Gibran's first exhibition of drawings at his studio in Boston, where he met the woman who would become his lifelong patron and supporter, Mary Elizabeth Haskell, a headmistress at a Boston private school. With Haskell's help (she would support Gibran financially and artistically until his death in 1931 and also helped edit his writing when he first published in English), Gibran went to study art with the sculptor Auguste Rodin in Paris from 1908 to 1910 and eventually settled in New York in 1912.

In New York, Gibran painted but also began to write. His early works were in Arabic and, after 1918, in English. His first published work, *The Madman*, came out in 1918; it was a book of parables and a hybrid of poetry and prose, a form that would mark most of his literary output. It was followed by *The Forerunner* in 1920. In 1923, he published *The Prophet*, the book that would become his most famous work. It was followed by *Sand and Foam* (1926). In 1928, *Jesus, the Son of Man* was published. It portrays the life of Jesus and its human rather than supernatural aspects and reflects the inspiration Gibran drew from the teachings of Christ. His final book, *The Earth Gods*, came out in 1931.

Though Gibran primarily became famous through his literary work, his development as a visual artist was equally productive and prolific. From an early age, he showed a love and talent for drawing. In New York, his studio, which he called The Hermitage, was filled with his artwork. He worked with wash drawings and paintings and remained faithful to a symbolist style consisting mainly of naked human bodies in an abstracted setting. He illustrated many of his books with his own drawings.

Gibran died in New York City on April 10, 1931, from cirrhosis of the liver and tuberculosis. He had been in bad health for many years, mainly from excessive drinking. Before his death, Gibran expressed the wish to be buried in Lebanon. The request was fulfilled in 1932, when Mary Haskell and Gibran's sister Marianna purchased the Mar Sarkis Monastery in Lebanon, which has since become the Gibran Museum. Gibran willed the contents of his New York studio to Mary Haskell, who donated her personal collection of nearly 100 original Gibran works of art to the Telfair Museum of Art in Savannah, Georgia, in 1950. Haskell's gift to the Telfair is the largest public collection of Gibran's visual art in the country and consists of numerous works on paper rendered in the artist's lyrical symbolist style.

Arab Romanticism

Gibran initially wrote only in Arabic, and his writings were part of an avant-garde Arabic version of romanticism, a movement initiated by Gibran in New York. He founded and helped to lead the New York Pen League or "Arrabitah," an Arab-American literary movement that began in the 1920s and included other important writers from Syria and Lebanon, including Ameen Rihani, Elia Abu Madi, and Mikhail Naimy. The Pen League's mission was to break the rules of Arabic literature in terms of language, meter, and rhythm. Gibran sought to free the tradition of Arabic literature from its archaic conventions and drew inspiration from the romanticism of the English poets of a century earlier. In the same way that Blake, Wordsworth, and Shelley aimed to create a new visionary language of expression, Gibran and his colleagues wanted to write poetry that challenged the classical forms of Arabic verse. They sought a poetic form that was more emotional and subjective.

The manifesto of the Pen League spoke of a more direct, clear expression that comes more from the heart than from tradition:

> Not everything that parades as literature is literature; nor is every rimester a poet. The literature we esteem as worthy of the name is that only which draws its nourishment from Life's soil and light and air. . . . And the man of letters is he who is endowed with more than the average mortal's share of sensitiveness and taste, and the power of estimation and penetration together with the talent of expressing clearly and beautifully whatever imprints Life's constant waves leave upon his soul.

The writers considered part of the New York movement were far enough removed from their native lands that they were able to successfully alter and redefine traditional literary tastes. At the same time, the movement was linked to a rise in Arab nationalism—specifically, Syrian independence from the Ottoman Empire. The new, more accessible and freer style of poetry was seen as a means of ushering in political change in the Arab world. Arab writers who settled in the United States were influenced by the values of freedom and democracy but at the same time rejected what they saw as the nation's excessive materialism at the expense of spirituality.

Although Gibran became increasingly less political through the years, in 1920 he wrote a poem titled "Your Lebanon and Mine," the publication of which was banned by the Syrian government. In the poem, Gibran contrasts the Lebanon he envisions, of natural beauty and peace among its people, with the Lebanon he knew, a place of politics and violence that he describes as the "chess game" between church and state:

> What will you leave for Lebanon and her sons a hundred years from today? Tell me, what will you leave for the future save pretence, falsehood, and stupidity?

> Truly I say to you that the olive sapling planted by the villager at the
> foot of the mountain in Lebanon will outlast your deeds and achieve-
> ments. And the wooden plough drawn by two oxen over the terraces of
> Lebanon outglories your hopes and ambitions.

Gibran experimented by writing in a hybrid form of prose poetry, a new
genre that further freed him from the established poetic practices and traditions of Arabic writing. He also started to advocate the role of poets and artists
in developing human consciousness and helping the individual access a more
divine realm.

Gibran read and was inspired by American transcendentalists such as Walt
Whitman, Ralph Waldo Emerson, and Henry David Thoreau. He was especially
interested in the American ideal of self-reliance and the idea of a greater self that
each individual is able to grow into. He believed that human beings are able to
progress toward a divine world and considered the metaphysical realm the key to
understanding the world and discovering more complex truths involving human
existence. His accessible subject matter and the fact that he published increasingly
in English rather than Arabic eventually brought him more of a Western audience
than an Arab one. However, he is nonetheless recognized as one of the founders of
modern Arab literature and a key member of the Arab literary renaissance of the
early twentieth century.

The Prophet
Summary and Analysis

The Prophet is a group of 26 prose poems that collectively present the impression
of a sermon delivered by a fictional speaker in an unknown time and place. The
prophet of the title is a character called Almustafa, who throughout the book gives
advice on various aspects of life: love, joy, sorrow, work, and death. Almustafa has
lived in the foreign city of Orphalese for 12 years and, in the first poem, is about to
board a ship that will carry him home. Before leaving, he is stopped and asked to
speak on the human condition and various aspects of living.

In the opening poem, "The Coming of the Ship," the seeress Almitra asks him
to stay and share his wisdom:

> Prophet of God, in quest of the uttermost, long have you searched the
> distances for your ship.
> And now your ship has come, and you must needs go.
> Deep is your longing for the land of your memories and the dwelling
> place of your greater desires; and our love would not bind you nor our
> needs hold you.

Yet we ask ere you leave us, that you speak to us and give us of your truth.

. . . .

Now therefore disclose us to ourselves, and tell us all that has been shown you of that which is between birth and death.

In this way, the book is set up as a parable or fable, an ideal vehicle for presenting the various religious overtones. God is often invoked, not in relation to a specific god associated with a particular religion, but in the sense of an absolute being, an essence that is present in every person. Love, Gibran asserts, is the essence of God in man:

When you love you should not say, "God is in my heart,"
but rather, "I am in the heart of God."
And think not you can direct the course of love, for love, if
it finds you worthy, directs your course.

The prophet's overriding and unifying message consistently returns to love. In each case, the love that he writes about resembles the Sufi concept of love as being a means of accessing the divine. Sufism is a general term for the mystical branches of Islam that absorbed Christian and other influences through the centuries. According to its tenets, marriage, for example, is not to be held tightly or owned, nor are children:

Love one another, but make not a bond of love:
Let it rather be a moving sea between the shores of your souls.

. . . .

Give your hearts, but not into each other's keeping.
For only the hand of Life can contain your hearts.

. . . .

children are not your children.
They are the sons and daughters of Life's longing for itself.
They come through you but not from you,
And though they are with you yet they belong not to you.

Gibran writes from a distinctly antimaterialist point of view. Just as human relationships are not to be owned, neither are possessions: "You give but little you give of your possessions. / It is when you give of yourself that you truly give. / For what are your possessions but things you keep and guard for fear you may need them tomorrow?"

Love is woven into every aspect of life, according to the prophet. The utopian ideal of love is seen even in the work an individual performs:

Always you have been told that work is a curse and labour a misfortune.
But I say to you that when you work you fulfil a part of earth's furthest
dream, assigned to you when that dream was born,
And in keeping yourself with labour you are in truth loving life,
And to love life through labour is to be intimate with life's inmost
secret.

The idea of a "god-self" is introduced by the prophet when he speaks about
crime and punishment. In introducing the concept, Gibran invokes a Buddhist
sensibility, the notion that, in a universe in which everything is connected, an
individual element or part of the world cannot be harmed without affecting the
whole. In this way, no one is a stranger, and even the ocean and the sun are part
of this "god-self":

Like the ocean is your god-self;
It remains forever undefiled.
And like the ether it lifts but the winged.
Even the sun is your god-self;

However, since people contain not only aspects of the god-self but also aspects of
the human, "so the wicked and the weak cannot fall lower than the lowest which
is in you also." As Gibran asserts later in the same chapter, "the corner-stone of the
temple is not higher than the lowest stone in the foundation."

In another chapter, "On Freedom," Gibran presents a paradox that centers on
breaking free of a metaphorical, inner prison. He writes that the idea of freedom is
not contained in a lack of burden or connection but is, in fact, an evolving process
and awareness, a chain of our own making:

Verily all things move within your being in constant half embrace, the
desired and the dreaded, the repugnant and the cherished, the pursued
and that which you would escape.
These things move within you as lights and shadows in pairs that cling.
And when the shadow fades and is no more, the light that lingers becomes a shadow to another light.
And thus your freedom when it loses its fetters becomes itself the fet-
ter of a greater freedom.

In the same sense, just as the concept of freedom is of our own devising, Gibran writes of pain as being largely brought on by the self: "Much of your pain is
self-chosen. / It is the bitter potion by which the physician within you heals your
sick self." The remedy, the prophet says, is silence and tranquility.

The self, according to the prophet, is a "sea boundless and measureless." In
order to know the self, Gibran offers this poetic musing:

Your hearts know in silence the secrets of the days and the nights.
But your ears thirst for the sound of your heart's knowledge.
You would know in words that which you have always known in thought.
You would touch with your fingers the naked body of your dreams.

This boundless self comes up repeatedly throughout the book. In speaking about time, he says, "And that which sings and contemplates in you is still dwelling within the bounds of that first moment which scattered the stars into space." In Gibran's world, love is boundless, "undivided and spaceless," and even one's own death is part of a process, a movement closer to the divine:

For what is it to die but to stand naked in the wind and to melt into the sun?
And what is it to cease breathing, but to free the breath from its restless tides, that it may rise and expand and seek God unencumbered?

At the end of the book, Almustafa closes his farewell address by saying, "A little while, a moment of rest upon the wind, and another woman shall bear me." This image reflects the romantic vision of eternal rebirth, reincarnation, and the continuity of life. These themes support and define Gibran's overriding vision of unity and the individual movement to greater wisdom, awareness, and enlightenment.

Major Themes

Reconciliation of Christianity and Islam

In *The Prophet* and other writings, Gibran developed the belief that behind all religions there are universal truths. He sought to merge the Sufi Muslim tradition (which advocated a direct relationship to the divine) with his Christian mystical heritage. Almustafa, the prophet in the book, can be seen as both a Christ figure as well as the universal man of Muslim civilization. In linking two different spiritual traditions, he seeks to highlight the similarities rather than the differences.

Robin Waterfield, in his biography of Gibran, wrote that *The Prophet*'s greatest success was that it came along at the perfect time and place, when the fusion of poet and prophet was most needed in the West: "He was the right person in the right place at the right time to bridge the gap between Western and Arabic literature in terms of both form and content. He was also the right person at the right time to bridge the gap as an Eastern prophet speaking with tantalizing clarity to the West." Sales of the book consistently doubled every year after its initial publication, and even in the midst of the Depression years, the book continued to sell well. By the 1960s and 1970s, as the work became a half century old, it was selling 5,000 copies a week in the United States.

The main reason cited for its overwhelming success is that its message is simple and overwhelmingly optimistic: Each person's life is greater than she or he knows, and each individual contains everything she or he needs for fulfillment and self-realization. In many ways, Gibran anticipated the so-called new age movement of the 1960s and 1970s, and the self-help movement that has emerged roughly in the past 40 years. Today, passages from *The Prophet* are often read at weddings, baptisms, and funerals throughout the world, attesting to the work's universal appeal.

The Prophet as Gibran

Many writers have argued that the prophet Almustafa is an alter ego for Gibran, in that the character's exile and desire to return to his native land is similar to Gibran's own longing to return to Lebanon. Gibran certainly had a desire for a transcendent homeland, as is evident in his earlier poem, "Your Lebanon and Mine." Scholars have written of the parallels between the book and Gibran's personal life. Besides Almustafa being linked to Gibran, the seeress Almitra is seen as Gibran's friend and benefactress Mary Haskell, and the city of Orphalese is New York. In addition, just as Almustafa has been exiled in Orphalese for 12 years, Gibran was likewise in New York for 12 years at the time of the book's publication. More than the personal details, Gibran's impassioned spirit comes through in the book's message. However, unlike the prophet, Gibran's own sense of his tortured self was more complicated and layered. Though he wrote to Haskell that it was crucial for him to live in compliance with the words that he wrote, according to Waterfield, "the gap between the man and the myth grew increasingly wide. The man was insecure, worldly, sexual; the myth projected a knowledgeable, ascetic prophet."

All the same, Mary Haskell wrote her own prophecy about this influential book in a letter to Gibran, on the day of its publishing:

> This book will be held as one of the treasures of the English literature. And in our darkness and in our weakness we will open it, to find ourselves again and the heaven and earth within ourselves. Generations will not exhaust it, but instead generation after generation will find in the book what they would fain be, and it will be better and better loved as men grow riper and riper. It is the most loving book ever written. . . . More and more will love you as years go by, long, long after your body is dust.

MALCOLM X

Biography

MALCOLM X WAS born Malcolm Little in Omaha, Nebraska, in 1925, to a Baptist preacher father and a homemaker mother of eight. Malcolm's father preached in support of black nationalism (which advocated black unity and independence from white governance and culture) and was a follower of the Pan-Africanist Marcus Garvey. The outspoken preaching of Little's father raised the ire of the Ku Klux Klan and forced the family to relocate several times, eventually moving to Lansing, Michigan. In 1929, the Little home was burned to the ground. Two years later, when Malcolm was six years old, his father's body was found brutally mutilated. Though authorities ruled his death an accident, local white supremacists were suspected of the murder. Malcolm's mother tried to support the family but eventually suffered a breakdown and was committed to a mental institution by the time Malcolm was 13 years of age. Malcolm and his siblings were divided into foster families and orphanages, and his mother never recovered.

The man who would become Malcolm X was forever shaped by these early events, in which race and prejudice served as signposts for the issues that would define the rest of his life. Though Malcolm proved to be a good student, he was discouraged early on from his wish to become a lawyer because of his race. He dropped out of high school and moved to Boston, in 1941, to live with his half-sister, Ella. There, he became involved in the cultural and social life of the predominantly black neighborhood of Roxbury, working odd jobs and getting an education in the street life of gambling, drugs, and prostitution. In 1943, he moved to Harlem, in New York City, where he cobbled together an existence and found himself in the middle of the heyday of the swing era. Back in Boston, he eventually formed a burglary ring, and in 1946, he was arrested and sentenced to 10 years in prison.

and replace it with an *X*—to signify his lost African surname. Proving himself to be an articulate spokesman for the Nation of Islam, he soon became a minister and showed a particular talent for converting black Americans in droves. He also founded new mosques in Detroit, Harlem, Boston, and Philadelphia.

Because of his charismatic presence and dynamic style of public speaking, within several years he was essentially the national spokesman for the Nation of Islam. With the rise of the civil rights movement in the late 1950s and early 1960s, he became a national media sensation as he advanced the Black Muslims' more radical form of politics. His rise in national stature came with a cost, however; Elijah Muhammad grew resentful of his fame and star power, and by 1963, the rift in the Nation of Islam became more apparent. Malcolm became increasingly disenchanted with Elijah Muhammad, after it was revealed that the leader had been involved with young women in the movement and had several illegitimate children by them. When Malcolm made a controversial comment after the Kennedy assassination, he was officially silenced by the Nation of Islam and barred from speaking for 90 days.

Eventually, Malcolm realized how deep the rift had become when he got word that Elijah Muhammad had been marked for assassination within the Nation of Islam. Malcolm renounced his association with Muhammad and soon thereafter went on a *hajj,* the traditional Muslim pilgrimage to Mecca. That trip proved to be yet another turning point for Malcolm, as it marked the first time he was directly exposed to the authentic Islam religion. He found himself praying side by side with Muslims of all backgrounds and origins and felt a kinship with even the "blond-haired, blue-eyed" worshippers. After returning to the United States, he spoke of a new developing perspective that tempered or softened his former conviction that white people were inherently bad.

Malcolm X's contributions as a civic and spiritual leader were tragically cut short on February 21, 1965. While speaking in front of an audience at the Audubon Ballroom, he was shot onstage and pronounced dead shortly thereafter. He was 39 years old. Three gunmen were arrested and convicted, all members of the Nation of Islam. Malcolm X's funeral in Harlem drew 1,500 mourners. Martin Luther King Jr. sent a telegram to Malcolm's widow, Betty Shabazz:

> While we did not always see eye to eye on methods to solve the race problem, I always had a deep affection for Malcolm and felt that he had a great ability to put his finger on the existence and the root of the problem. He was an eloquent spokesman for his point of view and no one can honestly doubt that Malcolm had a great concern for the problems we face as a race.

Malcolm X's legacy continues to this day, in large part due to his autobiography, written by Alex Haley, as told to him through conversations the two had and published posthumously in 1965. *Time* magazine later named *The Autobiography* of *Malcolm X* as one of the ten most important nonfiction books of the twentieth century. Countless book-length works, films, and documentaries have followed. Interest in his life renewed following the 1992 release of the Spike Lee film *Malcolm X*, which was based on the autobiography. Controversial during his own time and continuing to spark new debate and speculation after his death, Malcolm X looms large in the history of civil rights and American race relations and is remembered just as significantly for his contributions as a Muslim American.

The Autobiography of Malcolm X

Summary

The Autobiography of Malcolm X, published in 1965 after the Muslim leader's death, is a unique collaboration between Alex Haley and Malcolm X. Written by Haley and based on thousands of hours of conversation between the two men held in the last few years of Malcolm's life, like any memoir or autobiographical account, the book raises questions of authorship and accuracy. The book, like his life, was tragically cut short with his assassination in 1965. His early death left in its wake only speculation as to what path Malcolm X would have taken in later years.

The book can be divided in four distinct sections: Malcolm's formative years and childhood in Michigan; his years as a hustler and small-time criminal in Boston and New York; his conversion to Islam in prison and subsequent involvement in the Nation of Islam; and his break from Elijah Muhammad and development of an independent philosophy apart from the Nation of Islam. Structured in this way, the book presents Malcolm's life as a series of metamorphoses and evolving awarenesses and calls to action.

Major Themes and Analysis

Early Childhood and Formative Years

Malcolm's early years were spent in the midst of a large family—eight siblings in all—and an overworked mother, who was often at odds with her traveling preacher husband. His early sense of skin color and appearance stemmed from the varying ways his parents viewed and treated him. Malcolm felt that while his father favored his son due to his lighter skin, his mother was harder on him because of it. (Malcolm speculates that this was because his mother was the product of a white man raping a black woman in the British West Indies and that her resentment was due to this fact.) The other aspect of his early years was Malcolm's ability to speak out, to make himself heard in his large family with limited means. As he states in the book, "I learned early on that crying out in protest could accomplish things . . . if you want something, you had better make some noise."

The first major event—and trauma—for Malcolm occurs with the brutal death of his father and its effect on the family. In 1931, his father walks out after an argument with his mother, never to return again. His body is found later that night, almost cut in half by a streetcar and the skull crushed in. It was rumored that he had been attacked by white supremacists and then laid on the tracks to be run over. The trauma of the father's death for the family was only made worse by its aftereffects. The life insurance company that his father had bought a policy from refused to pay, claiming it was a suicide. Eventually Malcolm's mother, unable to support the family, began taking welfare checks from the state. The family lived in such extreme poverty that the children were "so hungry we were dizzy. My mother would boil a big pot of dandelion greens, and we would eat that. I remember that some small-minded neighbor put it out, and children would tease us, that we ate 'fried grass.'"

Malcolm's mother was proud and thus devastated to be "on relief." State agency officials began visiting the family more often, sowing the seeds of separation among the children. As Malcolm's mother's condition deteriorated, state agents sent the children to foster homes one by one. Finally, the court ordered her to be committed to the state mental hospital, where she remained for the next 26 years. At one point when Malcolm visited her there, she did not recognize him at all, which was too much for him to bear. He never visited her there again and later remarked that "I have rarely talked to anyone about my mother, for I believe that I am capable of killing a person, without hesitation, who happened to make the wrong kind of remark about my mother."

It was Malcolm's belief that the state in many ways was responsible for the disintegration of his family.

> I truly believe that if ever a state agency destroyed a family, it destroyed ours. . . . I knew I wouldn't be back to see my mother again because it could make me a very vicious and dangerous person—knowing how they had looked at us as numbers and as a case in their book, not as human beings. . . . Hence I have no mercy or compassion in me for a society that will crush people, and then penalize them for not being able to stand up under the weight.

His early exposure to white people—who presumably killed his father out of racial hatred and then furthered his mother's mental breakdown in their administrative indifference—was rooted in psychological trauma. These experiences laid the groundwork for his belief later in life that white people were "devils."

Boston and Harlem: Swing Era Youth

Though Malcolm was a bright student who showed promise, he dropped out of school and eventually made his way east to Boston, where his half-sister, Ella, lived. He was exposed for the first time to a neighborhood that was almost entirely black, where he soaked up the culture of swing and found his first job as a shoeshine boy at the Roseland Ballroom. He learned there that "everything in the world is a hustle," and before long he was deep in the world of the swing era. He "conked," or straightened, his hair with lye, bought his first zoot suit, learned the slang of the time, and danced the Lindy hop—all to fit into the style of the era and to distance himself from his unsophisticated Michigan roots. The first time he straightened his hair with the burning lye, he was pleasantly taken aback by the transformation of appearing white, but as he later remarks,

> This was my first really big step toward self-degradation: when I endured all of that pain, literally burning my flesh to have it look like a white man's hair. I had joined that multitude of men and women in America who are brainwashed into believing that the black people are "inferior"—and the white people "superior"—that they will even violate and mutilate their God-created bodies to try to look "pretty" by white standards.

Malcolm gets a job as a railroad cook and, by working the rails, makes his way to Harlem for the first time. Soon, he was hanging out at the Apollo Theater and the Savoy Ballroom, mingling with the likes of musical greats Dizzy Gillespie, Billie Holiday, Ella Fitzgerald, and Dinah Washington.

> Up and down along and between Lenox and Seventh and Eighth avenues, Harlem was like some technicolor bazaar. Hundreds of Negro soldiers and sailors, gawking and young like me, passed by. . . . In another two years, I could have given them all lessons. But that night, I was mesmerized. This world was where I belonged. On that night I started on my way to becoming a Harlemite. I was going to become one of the most depraved parasitical hustlers among New York's eight million people—four million of whom work, and the other four million of whom live off them.

Two years after arriving in Harlem, Malcolm was selling and using drugs, staging stick-ups and robberies, carrying a gun, and trying to stay one step ahead of the police.

By then, he had earned the nickname Detroit Red on the streets. He was what he called "a true hustler—uneducated, unskilled at anything honorable, and I considered myself nervy and cunning enough to live by my wits, exploiting any prey that presented itself. I would risk just about anything." Malcolm also finds himself running from "West Indian Archie," a numbers racketeer who is after him for supposedly cheating him. Archie had a photographic memory for numbers; Malcolm muses, "I've often reflected back upon such black veteran numbers men as West Indian Archie. If they had lived in another kind of society, their exceptional mathematical talents might have been better used. But they were black."

Eventually, of course, the hustling catches up with him, and he is arrested as the leader of a burglary ring in Boston. At the sentencing, Malcolm and his partner, Shorty, received more than the average burglary sentence, due to the fact that they were working with two white upper-middle-class women. At the end of this chapter, "Caught," Malcolm interrupts the narrative in order to state the meaning of his life story thus far:

> I want to say before I go on that I have never previously told anyone my sordid past in detail. I haven't done it now to sound as though I might be proud of how bad, how evil, I was. But people are always speculating— why am I as I am? To understand that of any person, his whole life, from birth, must be reviewed. All of our experiences fuse into our personality. Everything that ever happened to us is an ingredient . . . the full story is the best way that I know to have it seen, and understood, that I had sunk to the very bottom of the American white man's society . . .

Up to this point, Malcolm's life has been one episode after another of living by his wits, surviving but clearly making choices that are ultimately destructive. Stopping at this point to sum up his development thus far, he is careful to observe that, though his story is full of drama and interest, he is not telling his story to "titillate" but rather to serve a larger purpose. He is connecting his experience to the larger black American experience, an eventual fusion that gives the second half of his book—and his subsequent transformation into a national leader—all the more potency.

Revelation and Conversion

When Malcolm was sentenced to 10 years in prison in February 1946, he was not yet 21 years old. In prison, he became a number—just as his mother had become a number in the state mental hospital—stenciled on his clothing and eventually "it grew stenciled on your brain." For the first year of his incarceration, he spent his time in prison generally being an unruly inmate frequently sent to solitary confinement. For this behavior and his antireligious attitude, he earned the nickname Satan.

The first sign of change for Malcolm was meeting an inmate named Bimbi, who was articulate and educated and who encouraged Malcolm to take advantage of the correspondence courses the prison offered. Malcolm's education at this point had stopped in eighth grade, and though he could read, he could barely write, his penmanship poor. The second significant change was prompted by his siblings. Two of his brothers had written to Malcolm about "the natural religion for the black man." Nearly all of his brothers and sisters had converted to what was called the Nation of Islam. In Detroit and Chicago, this new religion had taken hold as an alternative to Christianity for blacks in the United States.

In 1948, Malcolm was transferred to Norfolk Prison Colony, an experimental rehabilitation facility in which instructors from nearby universities, including Harvard, came to teach. The prison also had an extensive endowed library containing thousands of books, especially on history and religion. Malcolm immersed himself in the books, at first reading "aimlessly, until I learned to read selectively, with a purpose."

Malcolm's brother Reginald came to visit him at Norfolk with the message of conversion, asking him "if a man knew every imaginable thing that there is to know, who would he be? . . . God is a man. His real name is Allah." This God had come to the United States, Reginald said, making himself known to a black man named Elijah, to sabotage the "devil" white man. For Malcolm, this message was a revelation:

> The white people I had known marched before my mind's eye. From the start of my life. The state white people always in our house after the other whites I didn't know had killed my father . . . the white people who kept calling my mother "crazy" to her face and before me and my brothers and sisters . . . the white judge who had split up the children . . .

Malcolm went through a period of great transformation after his brother's visit. The more he read about Elijah Muhammad and the Nation of Islam, the more he was convinced that his message was "the true knowledge," that the black man was the "Original Man" and that whites had usurped the great black empires and civilizations and cut them off from their own knowledge. Malcolm was "struck numb" by this message like it was "a blinding light."

Malcolm started writing daily to Elijah Muhammad from prison, and they began a correspondence that helped Malcolm continue his full conversion, to begin praying and following the rules of Islam. He was now like a hermit and came eventually to think of his former existence as belonging to another person altogether. Frustrated with his writing abilities, he increased his educational efforts in prison, obtained a dictionary and began copying every word, page by page. He eventually copied and learned the entire dictionary. He read as much as he could, and for the first time, as he improved his vocabulary, he was able to "pick up a book and read and now begin to understand what the book was saying. Anyone who has read a great deal can imagine the new world that opened." He read about world history but particularly about African and slave history, as well as the history of colonization. His world was opened, and his mind was challenged as never before:

> I knew right there that reading had changed forever the course of my life. As I see it today, the ability to read awoke inside me some long dormant craving to be mentally alive. . . . My homemade education gave me,

with every additional book that I read, a little bit more sensitivity to the deafness, dumbness, and blindness that was afflicting the black race in America.

Ironically, Malcolm realized that it was prison that enabled him to study so intensely, perhaps more than if he had gone to college: "Where else but in a prison could I have attacked my ignorance by being able to study intensely sometimes as much as fifteen hours a day?"

Malcolm's "homemade" education also enabled him to hone a skill that would serve him later: public speaking. With all his newfound knowledge, he began participating in the Prison Colony's weekly debating program. He found that he had a natural talent: "debating, speaking to a crowd, was as exhilarating to me as the discovery of knowledge through reading had been. Standing up there, the faces looking up at me, things in my head coming out of my mouth, while my brain searched for the next best thing to follow what I was saying . . . once I got my feet wet, I was gone on debating."

Ministering

When Malcolm was released from prison in 1952, he was 27 years old. He went to Detroit, where he lived with his brother Wilfred and started practicing Islam and attending the Detroit Temple Number One. Shortly afterward, he went to meet Elijah Muhammad in Chicago and was transfixed when he heard him speak. He also applied to change his surname to X—"the Muslim's 'X' symbolized the true African family name that he never could know. For me, my 'X' replaced the white slavemaster name of 'Little' which some blue-eyed devil named Little had imposed upon my paternal forebears."

After recruiting for the Nation of Islam for some months, Malcolm was named an assistant minister in 1953, and his charismatic preaching style proved to be immensely popular. He eventually quit his job at the Ford Motor Company and began to work full time to spread the teachings of Elijah Muhammad. He often used fiery language in his preaching to rouse and incite his listeners:

I want you, when you leave this room, to start to see all this whenever you see the devil white man. Oh, yes, he's a devil! I just want you to start watching him, in his places where he doesn't want you around; watch him reveling in his preciousness, and his exclusiveness, and his vanity, while he continues to subjugate you and me.

Every time you see a white man, think about the devil you're seeing! Think of how it was on your slave foreparents' bloody, sweaty backs that he built this empire that's today the richest of all nations—where his evil and his greed cause him to be hated around the world!

Malcolm went to Boston to preach and start a new temple there, then another in Philadelphia. He then returned to New York where the method for getting converts was to "fish" on Harlem's corners, especially near black Christian churches. Eventually, Malcolm was given a car to drive, so that he could continue his "fishing" for the Nation of Islam around the country.

Malcolm made a point of not getting close to the women who shared his faith, and his preaching was often biting toward women. As he says, according to Islam, "the true nature of a man is to be strong, and a woman's true nature is to be weak, and while a man must at all times respect his woman, at the same time he needs to understand that he must control her if he expects to get her respect." Though he tried to avoid marriage, he eventually decides to ask Betty X—without any romantic overtures—to marry him. They eventually have four daughters.

In 1959, a television documentary program was produced on the Nation of Islam called "The Hate That Hate Produced," which set off a firestorm of media coverage, both national and international:

> It was hot, hot copy, both in the white and the black press. *Life, Look, Newsweek,* and *Time* reported us. Some newspaper chains began to run not one story, but a series of three, four, or five "exposures" of the Nation of Islam. The Reader's Digest with its worldwide circulation of twenty-four million copies in thirteen languages carried an article titled "Mr. Muhammad Speaks."

Malcolm began appearing on radio and television programs to defend Elijah Muhammad and the Nation. He quickly picked up some strategies for arguing on air and getting control of the tone of the argument. His forceful, logical style would overwhelm and upset the other panelists. "Anyone who has ever heard me on radio or television programs knows that my technique is non-stop, until what I want to get said is said. I was developing the technique then." He also tried to anticipate what their counterarguments would be and come up with every possible answer to them. In this way, Malcolm set himself up as the mouthpiece for the Nation, though he is always careful to state that he is only speaking for the "Honorable Elijah Muhammad."

Break from the Nation of Islam

As Malcolm X grew increasingly visible to those outside the Nation, the seeds of dissent and envy were sown and a rift formed between him and Elijah Muhammad. According to the autobiography, there were a series of events that caused their eventual falling out. Ostensibly, the first outward sign of a feud between the two men was when Elijah Muhammad publicly silenced Malcolm for 90 days after an incendiary comment that Malcolm made after John F. Kennedy was assassinated (asked to comment, he said that it was a case of the "chickens coming home to roost"). However, Malcolm contended that he was silenced because of his growing popularity as well as for rumors circulating that Muhammad had had extramarital affairs with and children by various women in the Nation. This went against the strict Islamic moral code that they followed and was a severe betrayal to his followers. Even more grievous, in Malcolm's mind, was the fact that, rather than admit the truth, Muhammad chose to cover it up.

At first, Malcolm could not believe the allegations: "And so my mind simply refused to accept anything so grotesque as adultery mentioned in the same breath with Mr. Muhammad." He finally went to visit the women who had worked for Muhammad, and then became pregnant and excommunicated from the Nation, to hear the truth for himself. Malcolm felt increasingly burdened with this knowledge, and his growing doubt about the man he had loyally served for so many years. He also learned of Muhammad that in fact "while he was praising me to my face, he was tearing me apart behind my back. That deeply hurt me." Finally, when Malcolm was silenced, he knew his life was suddenly placed in grave danger:

> I hadn't hustled in the streets for years for nothing. I knew when I was being set up. Three days later, the first word came to me that a Mosque Seven official who had been one of my most immediate assistants was telling certain Mosque Seven brothers: "If you know what the Minister [Malcolm] did, you'd go out and kill him yourself." And then I knew. As any official in the Nation of Islam would instantly have known, any death-talk for me could have been approved of—if not actually initiated—by only one man.

Malcolm realized that the man who lifted him up from his situation in prison, who made him who he became, had betrayed him. His confidence and faith in the man was shaken, as he accepted the fact that Muhammad had covered up and tried to hide his own human weakness and failings from his followers. Malcolm determined that "after twelve years of never thinking for as much as five minutes about myself, I became able finally to muster the nerve, and the strength, to start facing the facts, to think for myself."

Pilgrimage to Mecca

After Malcolm split from the Nation of Islam, he decided to make a *hajj*, or pilgrimage, to Mecca. It had always bothered him that he had never experienced the religion as it was truly practiced in the orthodox Muslim world. Often Arabian, Middle Eastern, or North African Muslims would approach him saying that, though he seemed sincere in calling himself a Muslim, "they felt that if I was exposed to what they always called 'true Islam,' I would 'understand it, and embrace it.'"

The pilgrimage that Malcolm made after his break with Elijah Muhammad would prove to be the final transformation in a series of many changes in his life. It was on this trip that he realized the full extent and meaning of being a Muslim. He also realized how little he knew of the traditional Muslim rituals. Just as radical was his reassessment of the "white man." He learned that the racial descendants of Muhammad the Prophet were both black and white, and he felt the overriding unity of the people of all backgrounds who practiced the Islamic religion.

Malcolm wrote a letter from abroad explaining this transformation. In it, he spoke of the profound change he had experienced that brought about a new insight into America's racial dilemma:

> I have been utterly speechless and spellbound by the graciousness I see displayed all around me by people *of all colors*. . . . I have never before seen sincere and true brotherhood practiced by all colors together. . . . You may be shocked to hear these words coming from me. But on this pilgrimage, what I have seen, and experienced, has forced me to *re-arrange* much of my thought-patterns previously held, and to *toss aside* some of my previous conclusions. . . . I have always kept an open mind, which is necessary to the flexibility that must go hand in hand with every form of intelligent search for truth.

When he returned to New York, there was a large press conference in which Malcolm answered questions about his change in thinking. "In the past, I have made sweeping indictments of *all* white people. I never will be guilty of that again—as I know now that some white people *are* truly sincere, that some truly are capable of being brotherly toward a black man."

Malcolm's Final Chapter

In the last chapter of the autobiography, Malcolm appears to be a hunted man. He realizes that his days are numbered, that it is only a matter of time before the Nation of Islam is successful in their quest to kill him: "Every morning when I wake up, now, I regard it as having another borrowed day." Because of this growing awareness, his final days being interviewed by Haley are marked by a degree of retrospection or looking back: "I think, I hope, that the objective reader, in following my life—the life of only one ghetto-created Negro—may gain a better picture and understanding than he has previously had of the black ghettoes which are shaping the lives and the thinking of almost all of the 22 million Negroes who live in America."

What Malcolm seems to regret most is his lack of a proper education: "My greatest lack has been, I believe, that I don't have the kind of academic education I wish I had been able to get—to have been a lawyer, perhaps. I have always loved verbal battle, and challenge. . . . I love languages. . . . I would just like to study. I mean ranging study, because I have a wide-open mind. I'm interested in almost any subject you can mention."

The extraordinary life that Malcolm lived was a series of transformations and the circumstances that have shaped these changes. What emerges most strongly, though, is the portrait of a man with an engaged mind and the ability to look back and reflect on his past, in order to discern his own truth at any given moment. He was always trying to argue on behalf of that truth, but he was also flexible and curious enough to be able to challenge his own opinions and witness the evolution of his own mind.

In Alex Haley's epilogue, written in 1965 after Malcolm's assassination, Haley writes of how his relationship with his title subject changed over time. Haley started out trying to be "a dispassionate chronicler." However, he finds that Malcolm X was "the most electric personality I have ever met, and I still can't quite conceive him dead. It still feels to me as if he has just gone into some next chapter, to be written by historians."

SAMUEL HAZO

Biography

SAMUEL JOHN HAZO has worked in a variety of genres, producing poetry, fiction, essays, and plays. He was born in Pittsburgh, Pennsylvania, on July 19, 1928, to Sam and Lottie (Abdou) Hazo, who were Lebanese and Assyrian immigrants. After his mother died when he was a young boy, he and his brother, Robert, were raised primarily by their aunt. Hazo credits much of his curiosity for learning and writing to his aunt, who made education a top priority for him and his brother. He earned his B.A. degree from the University of Notre Dame in 1948. He then enlisted in the U.S. Marine Corps from 1950 to 1957, before returning to earn his M.A. in English from Duquesne University and his Ph.D. from the University of Pittsburgh.

Hazo is the author of 30 books of poetry and has published in many literary magazines and anthologies. He was a commentator and narrator on National Public Radio, KDKA, based in Pittsburgh, Pennsylvania. Hazo has received nine honorary degrees. He was appointed the first state poet for the Commonwealth of Pennsylvania by Governor Robert Casey in 1993 and held this position until 2003. About this position, Hazo stated, "My view of the role of a state poet is that he or she should strive to make poetry an expected and readily accepted part of public discourse. To this end, poetry should be an essential part of academic exercises, public events, and newspaper op-ed pages." As state poet, Hazo initiated the publication of a poem each week in the *Pittsburgh Post Gazette*'s Saturday edition.

Hazo is the founder and director of the International Poetry Forum in Pittsburgh. He is also the McAnulty Distinguished Professor of English Emeritus at Duquesne University, where he has taught for more than 40 years. He is married and has one son, Samuel Robert Hazo, who is an accomplished composer.

The Song of the Horse: A Selection of Poems 1958–2008
Summary and Analysis

The Song of the Horse is a collection that comprises 50 years of Samuel Hazo's poetry. Much of his poetry has direct relevance to his life. Some of the themes he focuses on include family, love, religion, war, suffering, and immortality. His work often reveals the importance of observation and the wonder contained in everyday life. The collection also offers the reader a sense of his development as a writer over the course of his career.

Major Themes

Concepts of the Self

In an interview from 1988 with David Sokolowski, Hazo remarked on using his own personal life as grist or possible subject matter for poetry:

> My view is that the self that Whitman was writing about [in *Song of Myself*] wasn't his little personal self, little Walt Whitman; it was the self that he perceived as being in everybody. That's a different self. If a poet can touch that, if he can go from the "private" to the "personal," I think that's what he should do.... I've written many poems where I am the second person, "you," when I mean "I." I mean the "I-you" that everybody can see. It's the you that's evoked when someone asks, "How do you start the car?" And you say, "Well, you take the key and put it in the ignition, you turn it, and then you put it in gear." It's all you, you, you, but you're speaking not of yourself but him and anybody else who's listening who wants to do it. So, my "you" or "I" in a poem is, I hope, interchangeable in that way.

This self that Hazo speaks about comes through in the poem "Ongoing Presences Have No Past Tense." In it, the sense perceptions of the body are what connect the speaker to the eternal self that Whitman evokes.

> I trust
> the body's unforgettable assurances
> that know what's true without
> discussion or hypocrisy.
> The teeth
> with just one bite can tell
> an apple from a pear.
> The tongue
> can savor at a touch what's salt,
> what's sugar.
> . . . .

> The eye
> does not discriminate, and everything
> in its complete democracy is ours
> in perpetuity to keep as near
> as here and dearer than now.

In a world that is uncertain, the body's experience is the only trustworthy source, Hazo seems to be saying. The "democracy" of one's perception is what keeps us rooted to the truth of reality. In "The Most You Least Expect," he uses the I-you relationship to conjure a self that is discovering its own existence:

> It's like
> your struggle to remember
> what you know you know
> but just can't quite recall.
> No matter how you frown,
>   the secret stays beyond you.
> You reach.
>   It moves.
>   You reach
>   again.
>   Again it moves.

Hazo often explores in poetic form the philosophical questions centering on how to live or forge a life. He is interested in the self in relation to time and how to live moment by moment, while observing the beauty of the everyday. In the poem "No Is the Father of Yes," Hazo grapples with our culture's negative tendencies and what is called "the infinite progression of the negative," in which negative thoughts feed on themselves. Hazo suggests we can choose and act otherwise:

> I make each day my revolution.
> Each revolution is a wheel's full
>   turn where nothing seems the same
>   while everything's no different.
> I want to shout in every dialect
>   of silence that the world we dream
>   is what the world becomes,
>   and what the world's become
>   is there for anyone's re-dreaming.

In making each day a revolution, he asserts that we can make the positive as infinite as the negative. The antidote, according to Hazo, is to observe one thing closely. He ends the poem by looking at a rosebush:

A single rose on that bush.
The whiteness of that rose.
                          A petal.
    of that whiteness.
                     The tip
    of that petal.
                 The curl of that tip.
And just like that rose
    in all its whiteness blooms
    within me like a dream so true
    that I can taste it.
                     And I do.

Language and the Art of Writing

Hazo frequently writes about language in terms of its exactness of expression. In the poem "Just Words," Hazo talks about words in various languages:

In Arabic a single word
describes the very act
of taking a position.
                     Greeks
pronounce three syllables
to signify the sense of doom
that all Greeks fear when things
are going very well.
                     As for
the shameful ease we feel
when bad news happens
to someone else, including
friends?
             In Greek—one word.

His admiration for language resides in its ability to express complex emotions and situations with precision and understanding. Language used in this way, as Hazo writes, "simplifies / and lets each word sound final / as a car door being shut / but perfect as a telegram to God." Hazo has also said this about language: "The fact of the matter is that language is how we perfect ourselves as human beings. If it is true that what you write or say is supposed to be as accurate a reflection of what's in your head or your heart as possible, then expression is very important. Which means that words are very important, both in their accuracy when used and in their degree of honesty."

In other instances, the struggle to find the appropriate words is what gives life to the art of writing. Hazo compares finding the right words to birds "swirling in a bluster of wings like a dream gone mad" in the poem "Breakdown." As the ancient Greek poet Pindar observed, when the rhythm changes, "the walls of the city will fall." This is the same thing, Hazo suggests, as when he writes and "the words won't perch":

> They swirl confused
> as any flock in flight.
> They're swirling
> now.
> I'm losing touch
> with what I should be saying,
> and I can't remember what I think
> I meant.
> The tempo's gone
> completely . . .
> Pindar was right.

The swirling of birds occurs when the tempo changes. It is the space between coherence or sense, when "madness rules the world," that the struggle to find words exists.

The writer's life is lived on the page, and Hazo seems to be a consummate poet. He is clearly content with his life's vocation. In "The Horizon at Our Feet," he discusses the writing life:

> My father said, "Your work
> is never over—always
> one more page."

Unlike his father, who was "a traveling man whose life / was always one more mile," Hazo chose to be a writer, "inking out your real future on white / paper with a fountain pen / and listening to what the writing teaches you." He finds this way of life to be both ordinary and sublime:

> But isn't living ordinary?
> For two and fifty summers
> Shakespeare lived a life
> so ordinary that few scholars
> deal with it.
> And what of Faulkner
> down in ordinary Oxford, Mississippi?
> Or Dickinson, the great recluse?

Or E.B. White, the writer's
writer?
        Nothing extraordinary
there, but, God! what wouldn't
we give for one more page?

Love

For Hazo, love is the most powerful force of all human emotions. He writes about it in a variety of ways, summoning romantic love, Christian love, and familial love. However, whatever the specific nature of love, Hazo is most interested in its immortal, unbounded form. In "Not Even Solomon . . . ," he conjures love in its eternal form and likens it to poetry:

        I'm talking love
and poetry and everything that's true
of each and interchangeably of both
        Randomly free, they leave
us grateful to no giver
we can name.
                They prove what cannot
last can last forever even
when we say it's lost . . .

Like the "troubadours / whose poems have outlived / their lives," love "turned them / into words that we can share / like bread and turn into ourselves." The specificity of love turns into a shared universal experience that everyone participates in and shares. Similar to Hazo's concept of the I-you relationship, love is an emotion that makes us human.

The love contained in marriage is what is invoked in "To All My Mariners in One." In this poem, the act of sailing together toward the horizon, where "nothing but the sun stands still," is what endures:

        We share the sweeter
alphabets of laughter and the slower
languages of pain.
                Common
as coal, we find in one another's
eyes the quiet diamonds
that are worth the world.
                        Drawn
by the song of our keel, what
are we but horizons coming true?

The sea is full of "blue mischief," but the stars are what guide them through, and they have "the wind for company." In this metaphor, the sailor's faith in his boat is what keeps the couple's love steady and true.

In another poem about marriage, "How Married People Argue," there is a more pragmatic view of love presented. A couple gets into a fight on the way to a party and postpones "the lethal / language they were saving for the kill / and played 'Happily Married.'" Faking their way through the civilized party of chilled shrimp and martinis, they only become real again when they are at home in bed.

> Word by word, they wove themselves
> in touch again.
>   Then silence
> drew them close as a conspiracy
> until whatever never was
> the issue turned into the nude
> duet that settled everything
> until the next time.

A married couple reconciles, knowing that "whatever never was the issue" has been temporarily set aside, until the next time they argue.

Death and Immortality

In the beginning of the poem "Morituri," Hazo quotes Italian film director Federico Fellini: "You don't know what you love until you've lost it." Love and loss are thus intertwined: "love's the legacy of loss / and loss alone." Hazo writes about death as being everywhere at all times, and we confront mortality "each time we breathe." In "Morituri," Hazo relives his brother's last days and death, trying to make sense of his life and passing. In the end, he comes to the conclusion that "Since brothers are forever brothers, / you're here and elsewhere all the time / for me exactly as you are / and always were—but more so."

Hazo writes about the fear of death and aging in "For the Dead, It's Over." He likens the process of aging and dying to being an actor in a play:

> Because the fear of aging
> makes us deal with death
> without a way of disengaging
> or pretending it's a dream,
> we always end by paging
> God to help us help
> ourselves and keep us waging
> our rebellion like an actor near
> the middle of the final staging

of a play that ends before
its time and leaves us raging.

The play he refers to is Shakespeare's *Hamlet*, and the poem echoes one of Hamlet's well-known soliloquies. The dead are at least spared "the fretting and the raging / that prevent us from surrendering / at last to sleep, or paging / through the past, or silencing / an argument we're always waging / with ourselves like Hamlet." Another poem that addresses the fretting actor onstage is the single-stanza poem "God and Man":

After casting the first act, checking sections
of scenery and mastering His rage
because the female lead blundered on page
one, He left the actors to themselves on stage
without a script and fretting for directions.

Rather than fret and rage, the antidote to fear, according to Hazo, is to be in the present moment. In "Who Promised You Tomorrow," he writes, "It's time / you learned that ears can taste, / and eyes remember and the tongue / and nostrils see like fingertips / in any dark." All that we know, the poem proposes, is acquired through the body's felt experience. Thinking of the American soldiers who died in France in World War II, he writes of their moment of death:

Before they left their bodies,
did they think of war or what
their bodies loved and missed
the most: a swim at noon,
the night they kissed a woman
on her mouth, the dawns they waited
for the wind to rise like music,
or the simple freedom of a walk
a waltz, a trip?

In several poems, Hazo revisits the theme of war and death, and he often calls on more recent events—the war in Iraq. In "Parting Shot," he presents poetry as a necessary balm in such times:

Some say that poetry has other
themes to sing about than that.
If that's the case, what good
is poetry that shies away from pain
and amputation?

> What else can make us
> feel, not merely know, that severed
> limbs and lives can never
> be replaced?
>> And all for what?

Hazo has a longer, more overarching view of war than reading the daily news would allow. One of poetry's functions is to make us feel, rather than simply know. Poetry has the ability to communicate the abstract, the unspoken, that which is difficult to express or phrase, and in doing so, it becomes essentially timeless and immortal. Poets still speak of the basic human emotions that individuals struggle to express. In "The World That Waits in Words," Hazo returns again to the comforting and healing or restorative powers of the written word:

> Deafened and dulled by the dead
> words of the living, I read
> the living words of the dead
> . . . .
>> I learn from them
> what lovers learn from love
> but find impossible to say.

The title poem of this collection, "The Song of the Horse," attempts to distill all of what poetry does in the single image of a running horse: "My father said, 'All horses / when they run are beautiful.'" The image of the horse running through history and war extends through the poem. Horses are also linked to poetry:

> Pegasus still says
> to gravity that poetry's none
> other than a horse with wings.

> It's not a question of intelligence.
> Horses, like poetry, are not
> intelligent—just perfect
> in a way that baffles conquest,
> drama, polo, plow,
> and shoe.

Horses are "poem-perfect" in the sense that, despite their utility, they run "just for the sake / of the running, the running, the running / they run . . ." Horses are so perfectly made that they will die even from a single fracture:

> So poem-perfect
> that a single fracture means
> a long, slow dying in the hills
> or, if man's around, the merciful
> aim an inch below the ear.

In this collection, Hazo makes a case for the existence of poetry as the form and expression—the song of the horse, as it were—that is most suited to bring us in touch with our humanity. In this way, poetry and the written word are among our most valuable and necessary tools in a fragile world.

AMIRI BARAKA

Biography

AMIRI BARAKA is a Muslim-American poet, essayist, dramatist, and music critic. He was born Everett LeRoi Jones in Newark, New Jersey, in 1934. His father worked as a postal supervisor and elevator operator, and his mother was a social worker. He studied philosophy and religious studies at Rutgers University, Columbia University, and Howard University, though he never obtained a degree. In 1954, Baraka joined the U.S. Air Force but was dishonorably discharged for suspicion of being a communist.

Amiri Baraka began his literary career as a beat poet and jazz critic in the Greenwich Village of the 1950s. In 1958, he founded Totem Press, which published such Beat icons as Jack Kerouac and Allen Ginsberg. The same year, he married Hettie Cohen, a writer and intellectual, and with her became joint editor of the literary magazine *Yugen* until 1963.

In 1965, Jones rejected his former life. He ended his marriage and moved to Harlem, where he founded the Black Arts Repertory Theatre and School, which promoted a black nationalist perspective on art, or art produced by blacks for blacks. In 1967, he married African-American poet Sylvia Robinson (now known as Amina Baraka). That same year, he also founded the Spirit House Players, which produced, among other works, two of Baraka's plays about police brutality: *Police* and *Arm Yrself or Harm Yrself*.

In 1968, he co-edited *Black Fire: An Anthology of Afro-American Writing* with Larry Neal. He also converted to Islam, changing his name to Imamu Amiri Baraka (Imamu means "spiritual leader") and assuming leadership of his own black Muslim organization, Kawaida. From 1968 to 1975, Baraka was chairman of the Committee for Unified Newark, a black united front organization. Baraka was a founder and chairman of the Congress of African People, a national Pan-Africanist organization with chapters in 15 cities, and he was one of the chief organizers of the National Black Political Convention, which convened in Gary, Indiana, in 1972 to establish a more unified political stance for African Americans.

In 1974, Baraka adopted a Marxist-Leninist philosophy and dropped the spiritual title Imamu. In 1983, he and Amina Baraka edited *Confirmation: An Anthology of African-American Women*, which won an American Book Award from the Before Columbus Foundation, and in 1987 they published *The Music: Reflections on Jazz and Blues*. *The Autobiography of LeRoi Jones/Amiri Baraka* was published in 1984.

Amiri Baraka's literary prizes and honors include fellowships from the Guggenheim Foundation and the National Endowment for the Arts, the PEN/Faulkner Award, the Rockefeller Foundation Award for Drama, and the Langston Hughes Award from the City College of New York. He has taught poetry at the New School for Social Research in New York, literature at the State University of New York at Buffalo, and drama at Columbia University. He has also taught at San Francisco State, Yale, and George Washington universities. Since 1985, he has been a professor of Africana studies at the State University of New York in Stony Brook. He is co-director, with his wife, of Kimako's Blues People, a community arts space in Newark, New Jersey.

"Somebody Blew Up America"
Summary and Analysis

Over the years, Amiri Baraka has often been provocative in his writing. Critics have charged that his writing is incendiary and divisive, and at times racist, homophobic, or sexist. Baraka wrote the following about his often-controversial writing and thought: "My writing reflects my own growth and expansion, and at the same time the society in which I have existed throughout this longish confrontation. Whether it is politics, music, literature, or the origins of language, there is a historical and time/place/condition reference that will always try to explain exactly why I was saying both how and for what."

In a 1993 interview with Maya Angelou, Baraka describes his passion for words as a political force, when he first discovered "their power to alter material life . . . a matter of being able to defend yourself." He explains:

When we grow up around music and oratory—you know, preaching—as we all do in the African-American community, we can recognize cultural utterance as a kind of style. I have always been fascinated with the style of language, with the force of language, with the kind of, if you will, emotional power—the power to define—language has. Language is a kind of historical monument.

In 2002, Baraka's appointment as New Jersey's poet laureate was revoked due to a controversial poem he published, "Somebody Blew Up America," soon after the terrorist attacks of September 11, 2001. This poem made the argument that Israeli officials knew about the attacks before they occurred:

Who fount Bin Laden, maybe they Satan
Who pay the CIA,
Who knew the bomb was gonna blow
Who know why the terrorists
Learned to fly in Florida, San Diego

Who know why Five Israelis was filming the explosion
And cracking they sides at the notion

Who need fossil fuel when the sun ain't goin' nowhere

Who make the credit cards
Who get the biggest tax cut
Who walked out of the Conference
Against Racism
Who killed Malcolm, Kennedy & his Brother
Who killed Dr King, Who would want such a thing?
Are they linked to the murder of Lincoln?

The poem is a long list that basically asks the question, "Who?" in quick succession, not only about the World Trade Center attacks but going back through the history of racism in the United States. The list of questions also takes up the issue of who possesses society's power and money:

Who make money from war
Who make dough from fear and lies
Who want the world like it is
Who want the world to be ruled by imperialism and national oppression
and terror
violence, and hunger and poverty.

Who is the ruler of Hell?
Who is the most powerful

Baraka speaks about his literary imagination as being framed in a Marxist foundation: "I'm still a Marxist, and I think it shapes my art in the sense that I am trying to get to the material base of whatever is going on—whatever I am describing, whatever event or circumstance or phenomenon I am trying to illuminate. I'm always looking for a concrete time and place and condition. I want to know why things are the way they are and how they became that way."

Tales of the Out & the Gone

Summary

Spanning the early 1970s to the first decade of the twenty-first century, this collection of short fiction is more poetry than prose, a hybrid of images and narrative. Introducing the collection, Amiri Baraka writes: "What should be obvious in these tales are the years, the time passing and eclipsed, the run of faces, events, unities and struggles, epochs, places, conditions, all gunning through and fueling them. Tales are stories—I like the old sound to it, *tale*. A story (where we have stored something) can be from anywhere and talk of anything. . . . The stories become tales when they can give us a sense of a less fully experienced dimension to what is."

Looking back on his time as an activist, Baraka is like a cultural historian, sharing his version of events in the same way that an African *griot* carries the collective memory of the tribe in an oral storytelling tradition.

Major Themes and Analysis

War Stories

The first section of short stories Baraka titled "War Stories." They span the 1970s to the 1980s and address the time when Baraka was actively involved in political organizing. Many of the stories in the section speak to the erratic, charged tenor of the time, both in the relationship between the organizers and the world at large and the relations among the political activists themselves. The narratives are called "War Stories" because they are, in Baraka's words, "taken from a life lived and experienced, from one kind of war or another. It could be the USAF in Puerto Rico, it could be the later Greenwich Village skirmishes, the Black Liberation Movement, or the Anti-Revisionist Communist Movement (we used to call it). Or what became post-all that." His war stories are not literal in nature, but they are "concrete results of real life that have or have not happened, or might have happened or might yet happen, or even metaphorical descriptions of different kinds of life conflicts that move us, whether we can speak of them or not."

His hometown of Newark holds a central place in these stories, and through it he tracks the trajectory of black nationalist politics during the peak years of the 1970s. In the story "New & Old," the infighting among the black nationalists is shown in a satirical light. The revolutionaries seem to have either become power-hungry insiders or have lost their direction and can no longer function: "Simba got worse, from the strain of revolutionary struggle. Began to swallow too many stay-awake pills and stay-asleep pills. Became a drowsy ordering vegetable. . . .

Amidst internal and external machinations, opportunism—a more exotic withdrawal from the real world."

The story "Neo-American" follows a day in the life of Tim Goodson, a fictional black mayor of a city not unlike Newark, as he prepares for a visit to his city by President Gerald Ford. Another character, Ray Sloane, is critical of the rise of a black elite emerging from the civil rights and Black Power movements. Once they acquire power, however, and become political insiders, they become more interested in serving themselves than bringing about social and economic change:

> And what we got here in this town? . . . black faces in high places, but the same rats and roaches, the same slums and garbage, the same police whippin' your heads, the same unemployment and junkies in the hallways muggin' your old lady. What is it? What is it? We strained to elect this nigger mayor, and what we got to show for it? Nothing but a burpin' black bastard slippin' his way around the city, sleepin' with fat ladies.

With the rise of the Black Power movement and the surge of black politicians getting elected, in Baraka's views, what they inherited was more of the same: "Nothing had changed." In support of this assertion, the problems of inner-city America in the 1970s are rampant in this story: "America in the 1970s, in the pit of depression called recession. One out of every four blacks unemployed, Finland Station the gut end of that. Thirteen percent of the whole nation unemployed, and in Finland Station it soared to thirty percent, fifty percent of the youth. And at nights there were more muggers on the streets than regulation folks."

The narrator of the story "War Stories" describes the idealism of the early days of political action: "A few of us believed that democracy for the assorted groups of colored, Negroes, and blacks could be won by refraining from eating meat and jogging, plus karate. An even smaller group of us thought that it might take more than that—maybe a little Malcolm, a little Che, a little Mao, some Ron Karenga, Carmichael, and pinches of some other folk, living and dead." The narrator compares the period of the 1960s and 1970s to his obsession with running, of feeling strong, motivated, and physically fit, "running free, so to speak." It was a period of "people pushing themselves, of ideals, of holding oneself up to measure against any number of arbitrary goals or models, convincing oneself, with small difficulty, that the world was the way we wanted it to be."

The political action committee in the story was formed to get black politicians elected. When the first black mayor is elected, the narrator remembers it being "the height of something. The pinnacle, the goal, whatever. . . . Hey, for a minute it seemed like I was brothers with all the people I could see. Like maybe even all the life and color that was inside me . . . could come on out. . . . That what was inside me could flow on out and mingle with all the other insides that could flow out." The conversational tone of the story is one of reminiscence or as if the narrator is being interviewed. Sadly, mirroring the loss of one's ideals, the narrator finally stops running in the park: "The park? The running, really. I miss that. Doesn't time fly? No, I don't run too much." The double murder of two black Muslims killed by fellow "renegade" Muslims, their heads found lying in the park's running path, is what finally curbs his idealism: "Yeh, the heads of the twin brothers were left there, blood still drying at the severed necks, right down by the lake. I think that's what killed it for me. I never went jogging there again." The story ends with violence signaling the end of an era.

Science Fiction

The second section of the collection is titled *Tales of the Out & the Gone*. More experimental and surreal than the first section, these stories have as their root elements common to the genre of science fiction. Baraka describes the title of these stories this way:

> In specific contexts, anything can be *Out!* Out of the ordinary. . . . Just as we might call some artist, like Thelonious Monk or Vincent Smith or John Coltrane, *Out!* Because they were just not where most other people were. So that is aesthetic and social, often both at the same time. . . . The 'Gone' could be seen or unseen or obscene. But even farther 'Out,' crazier, wilder, deeper, a 'heavier' metaphor, a deeper parable. We'd say that's 'way out.'

In the story "Heathen Technology at the End of the Twentieth Century," Baraka writes of an Orwellian time in which all metaphors will be wiped out and human brains will be unable to remember history: "When they discovered how to remove and imprison the mind (to make the brain unmetaphorical), dis/image it, there was a shrill whoop in the small laboratory." This is a humorous and nonsensical imagining of an American dystopia in which brains are switched with "naked murderer unisex supermodels arriving at certain peoples' houses like Jehovah's Witnesses." In this world, the United States is now called California:

> So then California (the name of the U. S. since 2019. Capital: Dallas) began to sweep metaphor out of citizens' minds large-scale. It was a major project. Every day the mounting aggregate of stolen metaphor metabolism was released with the stock market reports. The problem began when the collected metaphorical power collectively imagined nothing existed but what it could not imagine.

The logic on display in this story twists and turns and ends up completely confounding the reader. The world becomes one large blur, since "no one could be anywhere unless they didn't yet exist."

In another story, "Rhythm Travel," science is used to allow people to appear and disappear using music: "Your boy always do that. You knock, somebody say come in. You open the door, look around, call out, nobody there. You think! But then at once, music comes on. . . . Then you recognize what you hear, man. 'Aw, brother, you at it again. You in here, ain't you?'" In "Science and Liberalism (A Short Tale)," a record player is constructed that plays the listeners' voices back as music but will kill them if they are lying.

The science fiction in this collection derives from the image of a hip, urban African-American experience. In "Conrad Loomis and the Clothes Ray," for example, the title character is a chemist who creates a ray gun that instantaneously makes any kind of clothing the user wants. Conrad explains his invention this way: "Dig. Everything is, to some degree, a form of light. It's matter in motion— you know that. But it is, in essence, different forms and degrees of illumination. . . . So I can rearrange the light, and by doing this, recreate it as anything else it has the focus to become. The focus has to be supplied by the creator, the designer." His friend decides to order a leather coat "like no leather coat nobody ever had," thus becoming his own designer of fashion.

The problem with this invention is attributed to a problem with capitalism. A discussion follows in which the two men try to figure out the power dynamic of such an invention.

> You know, Conrad, everybody ain't gonna be thrilled with this. . . . And if some of those people find out, especially here in New York—the Garment District, remember?—then your ass will really be up against it. . . . It's a great invention, brother. But listen to me, these whatnots will not let you make no billions. They against they own folks other than them making billions. Don't you know that? It ain't really about race—it's about money.

In this way, though many of these stories are fantastical, Baraka is able to make a larger point about the economic conditions underlying the reality of this world.

As Baraka writes in the preface, "The stranger and more science fiction-like that the tales might seem, I hope they still carry a sense of what needs to be addressed and even repaired in the 'real world.'" For Baraka, writing fiction is his way of expressing his thoughts about the true workings of power and money. In his mind, fiction should "carry this kind of social presence, like a hymn of clear morality."

In many of these stories, the reader gets a view into Baraka's musical aesthetic. "A Monk Story" imagines the narrator running into a man in Newark who seems to be the jazz musician Thelonious Monk—one week after his funeral in New York. The narrator takes pleasure in the experience of his interaction with the mysterious figure of "Monk": "There was a kind of delight in it . . . the feeling there were millions of hip people on the planet. That we public hipsters were only the tip of the top. The number was out there rising. The I's of the Eyes who knows and hears.

Who dig the sounds. Who can understand the Dis and the Cover. Who love the classics, the masters, the ultimate live beauty of 'the music.'" (206) If Thelonious Monk is the master, in another story Baraka shows his distaste for another musician. In "Dream Comics," a character has a dream about Mick Jagger, to which his friend replies, "Mick Jagger! That corny, no-dancing, no-singing. . . . Man, you wasting your dream space on that clown." In the dream, he kills Mick Jagger and wakes up smiling about it. Besides being moral tales, these stories convey Baraka's aesthetic likes and dislikes. Two writers who inspire this collection are Octavia Butler and Henry Dumas; Baraka appreciates the fact that in their work "we see what they love and what they hate, what they think ugly and what they think beautiful." For Baraka, a voice is the writer's greatest gift, and it should never be meek or compromised.

NAOMI SHIHAB NYE

Biography

Naomi Shihab Nye was born in 1952 in St. Louis, Missouri, to a Palestinian father and an American mother. In high school, she lived in Jordan, Israel, and San
Antonio, Texas, where she also studied English and religion at Trinity University.
Nye began writing poetry at the age of seven. When she was 14 years old, she
visited her Palestinian grandmother for the first time, the person she has most
written about in her career, both in poetry and prose. Nye often writes of her experience as an Arab American from the position of a humanitarian committed to
peace and understanding between cultures.

Nye is the author of numerous books of poems, including *You and Yours*
(2005), which received the Isabella Gardner Poetry Award; *19 Varieties of Gazelle:
Poems of the Middle East* (2002), a collection of new and selected poems about
the region; *Fuel* (1998); *Red Suitcase* (1994); and *Hugging the Jukebox* (1982). Nye
has received awards from the Texas Institute of Letters, the Carity Randall Prize,
the International Poetry Forum, as well as four Pushcart Prizes. She has been a
Lannan Fellow, a Guggenheim Fellow, and a Wittner Bynner Fellow. In 1988, she
received the Academy of American Poets' Lavan Award.

Her poems and short stories have appeared in various journals and reviews
throughout North America, Europe, and the Middle East. She has also traveled
to the Middle East and Asia for the United States Information Agency promoting
international goodwill through the arts. She currently lives with her husband and
son in San Antonio, Texas.

19 Varieties of Gazelle: Poems of the Middle East
Summary and Analysis

19 Varieties of Gazelle opens with a poem that is an account of a bus trip through Oklahoma on the day of the attacks on the World Trade Center towers. The narrator of the poem is seated beside a man who has been released from prison that day—perhaps the only person in the country unaware of the tragedy that has occurred. It is a fitting beginning for the book, as the fateful day profiled provided many Americans with an excuse to demonize a culture about which they already harbored deep misunderstandings or erroneous generalizations. As she writes in her introduction, "September 11, 2001, was not the first hideous day ever in the world, but it was the worst one many Americans had ever lived. . . . For people who love the Middle East and have an ongoing devotion to cross-cultural understanding, the day felt sickeningly tragic in more ways than one. A huge shadow had been cast across the lives of so many innocent people and an ancient culture's pride."

Nye goes on to explain in the introduction that all her life she has "thought about the Middle East, wrote about it, wondered about it, lived in it, visited it, worried about it, loved it." As an Arab American, she feels that, along with other Arab-American writers, "we had all been writing parts of a giant collective poem, using the same bouquet of treasured images." *19 Varieties of Gazelle*, her grouping of new and collected poems, emerges as Nye's way of contributing to this evolving and growing poetic chronicle of the Middle East.

Nye uses poetry at this historic moment as a balm—"solace in the most intimate literary genre." She believes that in such times "we need poetry for nourishment and for noticing, for the way language and imagery reach comfortably into experience, holding and connecting it more successfully than any news channel." In these poems, she is speaking for her Palestinian grandmother, as a direct way of answering what Nye imagines is her grandmother's plea: "Say this is not who we are."

Major Themes
Food as Culture

One element that recurs in Nye's poems is the focus on food—figs, eggplants, bread, olives, cheese, coffee, and mint. As Nye says in an interview, it is not accidental that her imagery often centers on everyday things: "It keeps me focused on things close to us. The material world that gives us a sense of gravity. And that we'd like—we'd all like to be free to enjoy in our world." Food is found both in and on the land growing it and in the domestic spaces where it is prepared and eaten. Nye uses the imagery of food—and sense memory—to access and bring her closer to her Palestinian roots. The immediacy and universality of food brings the culture closer to the reader as well.

In the poem "My Father and the Figtree," she writes,

For other fruits my father was indifferent.
He'd point at the cherry trees and say,
"See those? I wish they were figs . . ."
At age six I ate a dried fig and shrugged.
"That's not what I'm talking about!" he said,
"I'm talking about a fig straight from the earth—
gift of Allah!—on a branch so heavy
it touches the ground.
I'm talking about picking the largest, fattest,
      sweetest fig
In the world and putting it in my mouth."
(Here he'd stop and close his eyes.)

More than speaking about figs, Nye's father is invoking in his memory the experience of his home. Further, he is trying to convey something essential about who he is to his daughter—his identity and connection to the earth of his native land.

Food and drink are often what bind people together as human beings in Nye's world. In "A Single Slice Reveals Them," a simple apple is a metaphor for revealing oneself in conversation:

An apple on the table
hides its seeds
so neatly
under seamless skin.

But we talk and talk and talk
to let somebody
in.

Even when language is not directly used, the act of consumption, such as drinking tea, becomes a ritual way of communicating and sharing common experience. In "The Tray," even in sadness, the regularity of drinking tea together unites the drinkers:

Even on a sorrowing day
the little white cups without handles
would appear
filled with steaming hot tea
in a circle on the tray,
and whatever we were able
to say or not say,
the tray would be passed,
we would sip

in silence,
it was another way
lips could be speaking together,
opening on the hot rim,
swallowing in unison.

In another poem, "Arabic Coffee," the ritual of drinking the coffee Nye's father serves is an opportunity to savor conversation and is thus a "motion of faith" that life can proceed civilly and sanely, despite war and violence. Even in the common act of drinking coffee lies the luxury of stopping and entering life more fully through a shared moment.

It was never too strong for us:
make it blacker, Papa,
thick in the bottom,
tell again how years will gather
in small white cups,
how luck lives in a spot of grounds . . .

when he carried the tray into the room,
high and balanced in his hands,
it was an offering to all of them,
stay, be seated, follow the talk
wherever it goes. The coffee was
like the center of the flower.
Like clothes on a line saying
You will live long enough to wear me,
a motion of faith. There is this,
and there is more.

This poem also reveals the passing of cultural tradition in the form of preparing food. As his children say "make it blacker, Papa," they are embracing the Arabic way of making coffee as their own, even if the beverage is being prepared in the United States and not in the Middle East.

An immigrant who proudly becomes a "regular" at the local coffee shop is the subject of "My Uncle's Favorite Coffee Shop." In this case, the experience of an immigrant being brought food by another, without having to say anything, is the ultimate pleasure:

Serum of steam rising from the cup,
what comfort to be known personally by Barbara,
her perfect pouring hand and starched ascot,
known as the two easy eggs and the single pancake,

without saying.
What pleasure for an immigrant—
anything without saying.

Food is not only unifying and essential to all for survival, it also serves as a specific indicator of a culture and a place. In this way, Nye uses both the universal and the particular to link us, the reader, to our own communal humanity. In an essay by Linda Strom and Lorraine Mercer, the authors note that "[Nye's] poems convey the idea that through observing the lives of others, we begin to dissolve the imaginary boundaries separating individuals, cultures, and countries. Nye's focus on food and its link to the histories of marginalized, often forgotten people underscores the notion that our connections to each other must extend beyond the boundaries of self and of geographical space." In the poem "Olive Jar," Nye gives us a view into the eating habits of Arabs everywhere in the simple act of eating olives:

In the corner of every Arab kitchen,
        an enormous plastic container
of olives is waiting for another meal.
        Green tight-skinned olives,
planets with slightly pointed ends—
        after breakfast, lunch, each plate
hosts a pyramid of pits in one corner.
        Hands cross in the center
of the table over the olive bowl.
        If any are left they go back to
the olive jar to soak again with sliced lemon and oil.
        Everyone says
it was a good year for the trees.

Later in the poem, while traveling to visit her family, she is questioned by an Israeli crossing guard about where she is going, who she is seeing, and who she will talk to. Despite this intrusion, Nye returns again to the image of the olives, as it is the sense memory of food that grounds her and connects her to her sense of humanity:

We will eat cabbage rolls, rice with sugar and milk,
crisply sizzled eggplant. When the olives come
        sailing past
in their little white boat, we will line them
        on our plates
like punctuation. What do governments have to do
with such pleasure? Question mark.
YES I love you! Swooping exclamation.

Or the indelible thesis statement:
    it is with great dignity
we press you to our lips.

War and Violence

Violence and conflict are for many a fact of life in parts of the Middle East. In Israel, where Nye's Palestinian extended family still lives, she tries to make sense of this reality. As an Arab American, she grapples with the distance that exists between this world and its inherent realities and the life she has fashioned in the United States.

In the poem "Going to the Spring," Nye brings up this difference in describing her cousins balancing huge buckets of water on their heads:

> They know there are countries
> where men and women kiss in the streets,
> where a man's hand on a woman's knee
> does not mean an earthquake . . .
>
> They know I can't carry the bucket.
> Still they offer it, grinning.
> They eat sour peaches and laugh
> at the way I look into things,
> as if there were something waiting there
> to be seen.

Nye gives the reader the sense that, in a constant state of war, life continues but often in a surreal or compromised state of reality. In the poem "Lunch in Nablus City Park," people have lunch while in the shadow of war:

> When you lunch in a town
> which has recently known war
> under a calm slate sky mirroring none of it,
> certain words feel impossible in the mouth.
> Casualty: too casual, it must be changed.
>
> What makes a man with a gun seem bigger
> than a man with almonds? How can there be war
> and the next day eating, a man stacking plates
> on the curl of his arm, a table of people
> toasting one another in languages of grace.

The woman across from her at lunch whispers, "I don't think we can take it anymore" and then, a few lines later, "A plate of *hummus*, dish of tomato, friends dipping bread." These contrasts point to the conflicting emotions and realities that surface in a life exposed to random violence, how one minute it cannot be endured and the next minute friends are sharing a meal together.

Nye struggles with what might have happened if she had stayed in Israel in the poem "For the 500th Dead Palestinian, Ibtisam Bozieh," a girl who is "Dead at 13, for staring through / the window into a gun barrel / which did not know you wanted to be / a doctor. . . . Had I stayed in your land, I might have been dead too." The girl in the poem was prominently featured in the media as being the 500th dead Palestinian, someone who would otherwise not have gotten any coverage but for the coincidence of the number. As Nye says in an interview,

> I was absolutely struck by that story and became haunted by thinking about this girl who lived in a village near my grandmother's, and about how innocent she was. I thought about how natural it is to be a curious 13-year-old girl looking out the window. She was all of us and this could have happened to any of us. I became obsessed thinking about her. I felt as if I had been with her after weeks of thinking about her. Later, I read that poem in Jerusalem and a Palestinian journalist wanted to print it in an Arabic newspaper. They were not allowed to print it by the Israeli censors.

Nye talks about how the experience of having this poem censored "was a haunting experience for me because suddenly I realized, with even more immediacy, what their lives had been like. The inability to even cry out in the event of someone's death is something that Americans have never understood all these years—how Arabs there were denied their voices and their basic human right to say things."

Nye offers her readers a window into what life is like for Palestinians in the poem "The Palestinians Have Given up Parties." She compares life before the Israeli-Palestinian conflict intensified to the aftereffects:

Once singing would rise
in sweet sirens over the hills
and even if you were working
with your trees or books
or cooking something simple
for your own family,
you washed your hands,
combed water through your hair . . .

Now when the students gather quietly
inside their own classroom
to celebrate the last day of school,
the door to the building

gets blasted off.
Empty chairs where laughter used to sit.
Laughter lived here
jingling its pocket of thin coins
and now it is hiding.

Religion

In the poem "Different Ways to Pray," Nye takes as her subject the various ways of being Muslim, the variety of expressions used while praying. Prayers by some women could be "weathered rib bones, / small calcium words uttered in sequence, / as if this shedding of syllables could / fuse them to the sky." Alternately, there is the shepherds' way of praying: "*Hear us! We have pain on earth! / We have so much pain there is no place to store it!*"

> Some prized the pilgrimage,
> wrapping themselves in new white linen
> to ride buses across miles of sand . . .
>
> While for certain cousins and grandmothers
> the pilgrimage occurred daily,
> lugging water from the spring
> or balancing baskets of grapes . . .
>
> There were those who didn't care about praying.
> The young ones. The ones who had
>   been to America.
> They told the old ones, you are wasting your time . . .
>
> And occasionally there would be one
> who did none of this,
> the old man Fowzi, for example,
> who bet everyone at dominoes,
> insisted he spoke with God as he spoke with goats,
> and was famous for his laugh.

Prayer, in the sense meant in this poem, is larger than the literal meaning of the word. Nye references a wider view of the sacred and, by describing these different spiritual states of being, is once again connecting to a larger awareness of humanity. Even the old man Fowzi has his way of talking to God.

In the poem "For Mohammed on the Mountain," Nye speaks directly to the Muslim prophet Mohammed as if he is her distant uncle, talking to him about her struggle to know him, and to understand religion:

Uncle Mohammed, you mystery, you distant
        secretive face,
lately you travel across the ocean and tap me
        on my shoulder
and say "See?" And I think I know what you are
        talking about,
though we have never talked, though you have
never traveled anywhere

As a child, she does not understand why Mohammed is on the mountain and wonders how he gets food, who he talks to, and what he does all day. By thinking of him as a real, living person, she is connecting to her father's religion as a child would, in a personal and immediate way. Later, when her family moves to Jerusalem, she looks for her uncle and cannot find him:

We came to your country, Uncle, we lived there
        a year
among sheep and stones, camels and fragrant oils,
and you would not come down to see us.
I think that hurt my father, though he never said so.
It hurt me, scanning the mountains
        for sight of your hut,
quizzing the relatives and learning nothing.
Are you angry with us? Do you think my father
        forgot you
when he packed his satchel and boarded the ship?

In a childlike way, Nye wonders whether they are part of the culture or not and what gets lost when you go away. She tells Mohammed that her father is, in fact, "closer to you than you know . . . you think he feels like an American? / You think he forgets the call to prayer?" The poem ends with more of a fully developed relationship with Mohammed, the speaker concluding that maybe he was not angry after all:

I have made myself a quiet place in the swirl.
I think you would like it . . .
As for friends, they are fewer and dearer,
and the ones who remain seem also to be
        climbing mounts
in various ways, though we dream we will meet
        at the top.
Will you be there?
Gazing out over valleys and olive orchards,

telling us sit, sit,
you expected us all along.

In the adult version, Mohammed is not angry with her; rather, he has been waiting for her to come and meet him there on the mountain.

The feeling of being a part of two worlds and two religions informs several poems in this collection. In "Half-and-Half," Nye describes confronting the more fixed view of religion as being one thing only:

> You can't be, says a Palestinian Christian
> on the first feast day after Ramadan.
> So, half-and-half and half-and-half.
> He sells glass. He knows about broken bits,
> chips. If you love Jesus you can't love
> anyone else. Says he.

Later in the poem, she refers to what is presumably her recipe for religion: a woman "is making a soup from shat she had left / in the bowl, the shriveled garlic and bent bean. / She is leaving nothing out." Nye is careful not to leave anything out in her own identity, and it is the "broken bits" that are important to her, not a religious doctrine expressed in absolute terms.

Again, in the poem "Two Countries," Nye brings up the question of people existing in separate worlds and going to places "larger than themselves":

> Skin had hope, that's what skin does.
> Heals over the scarred place, makes a road.
> Love means you breathe in two countries.
> And skin remembers—silk, spiny grass,
> deep in the pocket that is skin's secret own.
> Even now, when skin is not alone,
> it remembers being alone and thanks something
>   larger
> that there are travelers, that people go places
> larger than themselves.

Skin is personified as being the source of the body's sense memory in the poem. A person can heal just as skin heals or as nations might heal. In this way, Nye is optimistic when it comes to peace. She makes an argument in this collection that peace is attainable, no matter how long it takes. In the poem "How Long Peace Takes," she acknowledges the infinite nature of peace:

> As long as the slow crawl of loosening paint
> and the bending of slim wax tapers

As long as blue thread spinning
a vine of birds up one seam down the other
and the bodice don't forget the bodice
doubly thick with wings and hidden treasure

As long as my Sitti twists her hanky
around two small gold coins
in the bed   in the bed
and says she is not tired

As long as the bed
and all the people who slept in it

As long as the splitting of almonds
the stirring of lentils
the scent of marimea
and the Universal Laundry

As long as the question—what if I
were you?—has two heads

As long as the back of the skull is
vulnerable and the temple and the chest

As long as anyone feels exempt
or better and one pain is separate
from another and people are pressed flat
in any place

And longer

If every day the soldier slaps
another cousin's face

As long as we keep asking the question, what is it like to be another person, Nye seems to be saying, we will advance in the direction of peace as opposed to conflict. It is only through our connection to one another as human beings, and to our own specific and humble experiences, that we can override the tendency for violence. As this poem points out, however, we will always remain vulnerable to the slap on the face.

MONA SIMPSON

Biography

MONA SIMPSON was born in 1957 in Green Bay, Wisconsin, to an American mother and a Syrian father. Similar to the story in her first novel, *Anywhere but Here*, when Simpson was ten years old, her parents split up; she and her mother moved from Wisconsin to Beverly Hills, where Simpson eventually went to high school. She then studied English at the University of California at Berkeley and received her M.F.A. in writing at Columbia University.

She began writing *Anywhere but Here*, about a turbulent mother-daughter relationship, while still in graduate school. It was published in 1986 and was adapted into a feature film of the same name in 1999. Her second novel, *The Lost Father*, follows the same character from her first book, this time exploring the daughter's search for her father.

As an adult, it was revealed that Simpson is the younger sister of Steve Jobs, co-founder and current chief executive officer of Apple Computer, Inc. Jobs was placed up for adoption as a baby by their then-unmarried parents. Simpson's third novel, *A Regular Guy*, follows a character who bears a striking resemblance to her biological brother. The protagonist is a millionaire entrepreneur and technology business executive whose estranged daughter finds him and then has a hand in transforming his life. Mona Simpson's fourth book, a novella titled *Off Keck Road*, was published in 2000. Her newest novel, *My Hollywood*, is forthcoming.

Simpson lives in Santa Monica, California, with her husband and son. She teaches at Bard College. Apart from fiction, she also has written essays for various anthologies. She has received many awards, including a Guggenheim Fellowship, the Whiting Prize, and the Lila Wallace Readers Digest Award, and was nominated for a PEN/Faulkner Award.

Anywhere but Here
Summary

Anywhere but Here opens with Adele August and her twelve-year-old daughter, Ann, driving across the country, destined for Los Angeles. Mother and daughter have been fighting, and Adele kicks Ann out of the car and drives away, only to come back for her several minutes later. Thus begins the saga of a mother-daughter relationship that is fraught with dysfunction. This scene presents the irresponsibility of Adele's unconventional parenting and the strange dance of interdependency that exists between the two generations. While the novel follows the mother and daughter to California, Simpson also casts a backward glance to the family's past in Wisconsin, with twentieth-century America and its associated ideals and struggles serving as the backdrop to the action.

Simpson writes the book mainly from the first-person point of view of Ann. Though she is twelve years old when the book opens, the narrative looks back to a younger Ann and forward to her adult, postcollege years. The novel is intercut with chapters told from the perspective of Ann's grandmother Lillian and her aunt Carol. These additions interweave with Ann's viewpoint to give a fuller picture of the family dynamic and the complicated intergenerational relationships that affect both mother and daughter.

Major Themes and Analysis
Identity and the American Dream

One of the main themes of *Anywhere but Here* is the pursuit of the American Dream. Adele August, though unconventional by many standards, nonetheless values material objects and status more than authenticity and substance. Her obsession with cars, eating steak, shopping, television, and clothes aligns her with a distinctly American preoccupation with class and money. Throughout the book, her self-obsession and dependence on her daughter are explored through the lens of twentieth-century American life, with California, in particular, viewed as the desired destination and escape from the family's legacy and history in Wisconsin.

This focus on outward appearances, on playing the part of the ideal mother and daughter, puts a strain on Ann, who is forced to lie or support her mother's liberties with the truth. When her mother is lying, Ann has to play along. "I knew I shouldn't say anything, in case I contradicted my mother. I could tell she was lying, but I wasn't sure. And I didn't know why. She liked me to talk, around strangers, like a kid." Talking "like a kid" was in direct contrast to how often Ann was forced to act older than her years.

Adele August, though in many ways an irresponsible mother, in other ways is also a charming, sympathetic person. Her moodiness and mental instability keep Ann's life unpredictable, and even fun, at times. "Strangers almost always love my mother. And even if you hate her, can't stand her, even if she's ruining your life, there's something about her, some romance, some power. She's absolutely herself. No matter how hard you try, you'll never get to her. And when she dies, the world will be flat, too simple, reasonable, fair."

In the beginning of the novel, Ann is merged and closely identified with her mother to the point that they seem at times to be the same person. As a young girl, she notes that when she grows up, "I knew what I wanted to be: I wanted to be just like her." Though she fights with her mother often and can be as stubborn and willful as any child, Ann is more often identified with her mother than not: "The thing about my mother and me is that when we get along, we're just the same. Exactly." Ann even has the same likes and dislikes as her mother. On boarding a plane from Wisconsin after a tragic and sad family visit, she observes that "once we were in the air, we felt giddy. We both loved airplanes; they were like doctors; they made us feel rich and clean. We were dressed in our best clothes and new stockings charged at Shreve's. No one seeing us would know anything true."

On another occasion, Adele's mother observes, "That's one thing about us, Ann, we have taste. We can go anywhere and they'd think, Hey, what a great-looking mother and daughter. And that's class." For them, the American Dream means the freedom of movement and the freedom of self-expression, the right to discover who they are and to confront life on their own terms.

Escape and Reinvention

The version of the American Dream that is most powerfully evoked for Ann and Adele August—as a symbol of American success—is Los Angeles, California, specifically Beverly Hills. While still in Wisconsin, mother and daughter begin plotting their escape years before they actually leave. They use it as their collective fantasy to lift them out of their ordinary circumstances and inspire them to make the journey west someday. The dream of California is also the secret that bonds them together. "My mother and I made up a secret. . . . We decided we would go to California, but it was our secret. I knew I'd have to be different from other children. I'd have to be better than the other kids to be picked and make all that money." The dream is a conditional one, in that it is tied to the premise that Ann will get on television, become a "child star," and make them rich. When Ann is attacked by a pack of boys and they cut her long, dark hair, her mother's reaction is harmful to her daughter: "'I mean, it's what MADE you special. It was your crowning glory. You talk about going to California and auditions for television, well, let me tell you, other kids are cuter. You hair was what you had going for you. Without it, I just don't think you'll stand out.'"

In this way, California becomes an abstraction, a dream location, and an indication of how delusional Adele is as a parent.

> Sometimes it seemed years, it had been known between us, decided, we
> were going to California. But we'd never really said it. It was our secret, a
> nighttime whispered promise.... Spells can be broken by the person who
> started them. Some things, once spoken in the daylight, can never be the
> same. I didn't want to leave, but I didn't want to give up California, either....
> But if we stayed, we wouldn't have California anymore. We couldn't whisper
> at night about moving there when we were sad. We'd never believe it again.

Though it has been a dream and a vaguely developing plan for years, at this point Adele asks Ann to choose their future—either a Lincoln Continental or California. Though she has no idea what to do, she picks California, if only because the promise seems too appetizing and because she can see what would happen "to the people who stayed" in their midwestern town.

In contrast to their fantasy of California, the reality of being there proves to be a much harsher truth. When they arrive in California, they immediately feel isolated and alienated from everyone. "We didn't know how they could do it; live, eat, look like that. For us, it seemed so hard." When in Wisconsin, they felt attractive; but in California, compared to the throngs of appearance-conscious people, "we felt acutely aware of everything wrong with us." Ann and her mother "weren't the hits we'd hoped to be." Adele's job at a public school in Watts proves unbearable to her, and she quits after the first day. Ann remembers their reaction when she got word of the job in Wisconsin, a swelling pride that has since quickly evaporated. "We felt like dupes now, for having been proud. And she probably went back to thinking what she usually thought about herself, that she wasn't quite right in the world." Ann also has a hard time fitting in socially (and financially) at Beverly Hills High School, where all the other students immediately ask her what street she lives on and what her father does. The advice they get from a realtor they have met is for Ann to "'work it in the conversation that she's from Wisconsin. A lot of the new kids are just from other schools in LA and that's a bore. But Wisconsin's different, so see if she can mention that.'" This advice is perfect from Adele's standpoint, as she "loved social strategy, careful planning. It was one of her lifelong passions."

Even though the reality of California turns out to be a difficult, lonely, and insecure place for Adele and Ann, they both prefer the fantasy and appearance of it to the truth of Wisconsin. On their first trip back to the Midwest, to go to Ann's cousin's funeral, they notice the difference even on the plane from Chicago; the stewardesses faces "were not as delicate or chiseled as their counterparts' on the coastal flight . . . those voices, their nasal friendliness, sounded homely." Ann feels changed by California: "We seemed different, already. I didn't know what would happen to us. . . . We both felt terrified of landing." However much Ann feels changed, Wisconsin is still her home. When her mother gets into a fight with her sister and tries to leave, Ann hesitates at first:

The land—it was the same, only small, the trees seemed lower, the houses simple compared to those we'd seen. Still, I understood things here. I knew how to be comfortable. We weren't doing so well in California. . . . My mother called me again. Everyone waited. . . . I looked down at my legs, in dark pantyhose, good high-heeled shoes. The names and prices of these seemed like secrets I would be embarrassed to tell. I couldn't stay here. There was nothing. I'd be like my mother, always wanting to go away.

By deciding to follow her mother back to California, Ann is choosing a life of appearances and ever-illusive wealth and fame—as opposed to the roots and authenticity life in Wisconsin provides her.

Miraculously, after several years, Ann eventually gets cast on a television show. However, instead of it being the realization of a dream, she only sees the disillusion and fakery of it all: "Before, I'd imagined the movies were the center of the world, and people loved you, people like my father came up and saw you and told you you were beautiful. But this was like nothing. . . . We stood around waiting most of the time. Nobody thought we were anywhere." Outside the realities of the workaday world of television, other people were still enamored by it, however: "But other people, outside television, treated you different. Teenaged girls on Beverly Drive giggled behind, turned shy if I stopped, and looked up to me."

Men and Fathers

Another theme of the book is the pursuit—and absence—of men in Ann and Adele's lives. As Ann notes, "My mother's two passions were for difficult men and expensive clothing, neither obtained by the usual methods, but with a combination of luck, intuition and calculated risk." Her mother's search for a man who will protect them and materially provide for them is one of Adele's persistent pursuits throughout the book. As Adele often repeats to her daughter, "'Just remember, I'm the one who has to catch a man in this family. I'm the one who has to find you a father.'" Adele's approach is to be passive and manipulative, a tactic she often advises Ann to adopt as well: "be nice to him. Play up to him a little. I bet if you're real cute and quiet, he'll do it for you. . . . Just be real cute and make him *want* to help you. You've got to learn to make men want to do you favors." Adele's obsession with beauty and clothes can be seen as her way of gaining power over men and trying to "catch" them, rather than attempting to build a meaningful relationship based on love and respect.

Another male presence, Ann's father, comes up again and again between them in the novel. Ann's biological father is an Egyptian professor and failed vacuum cleaner salesman who leaves when Ann is still young. Adele tries in her own dysfunctional way to fill this absence and bridge the emotional gap. At one point, she tells Ann, "But, don't worry, because there'll be other men in our lives. I'll catch another father for you, you just wait. . . . I'll tell you, a father is someone who DOES for you and GIVES to you. Not just take, take, take. I mean, what makes your dad your father? Just a little sperm. And genes. What did he ever do for you?"

Typically, Adele's response to Ann's understandable desire to have her father in her life is selfish and inappropriate. When Ann brings up the issue of whether she misses her father, her mother tells her, " 'Honey, you didn't even know your dad. . . . How could you miss him? . . . I'm the one who misses my dad. . . . But you never had that real total love. Maybe you're lucky, you know, maybe it'll be better for you. You'll never know enough to miss it.'"

Three years after leaving, Ann's father calls them to ask if they can come to visit him in Las Vegas and go to Disneyland. Ann's experience of seeing her father is disappointing and strange. Before Ann and Adele go to meet him, he loses the money through gambling and cannot take her away after all, promising to take her on the next trip. Ann wants to connect with her father but cannot: "Suddenly, I wanted the name of a month, not to see Disneyland but to see him. . . . I wanted to say that I didn't care about Disneyland. . . . But I never said it. All I did was hold his hand tighter and tighter."

For all the disappointment, Ann is still enthralled by her father. On the plane home from visiting him, she fondly holds the cheap gift her father gave her. Her mother, however, harshly reminds Ann who her primary provider is: "I work, and I pay for your school and your books and your skates and your lessons. . . . A seventy-nine cent package of headbands."

Family Legacy

As a young girl, Ann does not question her mother or her mother's behavior. Despite Adele's unpredictable mood swings, like in any abusive relationship, Ann wants her mother to like her and works toward that goal. After a fight, Ann would always be relieved that "we were friends again, I was her daughter, she liked me. And I was relieved, happy in some recovered way."

The moments when Ann finds her mother "normal" are few and far between. When Adele seems to have an appropriate response to a given event, Ann finds that "I loved her then, she seemed so normal and reasonable. I thought now we might start living the way other people did." Ann's grandmother Lillian sheds some light on Adele and says about her daughter: "'Oh, there was always something not quite right about her. Something a little off. She wasn't quite all there.'" Ann has her own interpretation of her mother's behavior and character: "There was something about the way she said things, about the way she was vague—it made her always seem wrong. You couldn't be sure. It was hard to tell what my mother did and didn't know. She didn't use facts."

The complexities of family dynamics and the reasons why people end up acting and behaving the way they do are one of the novel's consistent if unanswerable themes. In the section narrated by Lillian, the older woman wonders why her brother left home many years ago. She tells the story of how her mother, Adele's grandmother, feels guilty about once kissing her son in a romantic fashion. Lillian reflects on the incident: "I still sometimes wonder whether that might have something to do with it. Because Milton always loved his momma, he loved her but he had to get away." Years and several generations later, Ann also finds herself having to get away from her mother because of inappropriate boundaries.

Lillian reflects as well on how different her two daughters were treated in the family. Carol was the older sibling who did not get as much and had to make do, while Adele was the spoiled one: "Everything Carol didn't get, Adele did. When I think of it, it makes me mad. Because we were older then and then we really wanted a child. We were the right age for one. And we had more money."

Disillusionment and Separation

As Ann gets older, the close relationship she has had with her mother starts to fade. She becomes increasingly more independent, as she begins to comprehend more fully her mother's instability. This desire for independence first surfaces when Ann is twelve: "I felt something then. . . . I wanted to get away from her. There was nowhere I could go. I was twelve. She'd have me six more years." Her experience gives her a wisdom beyond her years, in that she has to question her mother's authority and rely on her own judgment: "I believed and I didn't believe my mother. I was beginning to distrust her promises but I still believed her threats."

At one point, Ann gets into an argument with her mother and realizes for the first time that she is not as safe with her as she once thought. "I'd been taught all my life or I knew somehow, I wasn't sure which, that you couldn't trust the kind faces of things, that the world was painted and behind the thin bright surface was darkness and the only place I was safe was home with my mother. But it seemed safer outside now, safer with indifference than with care." Ann has slowly arrived at the painful realization that her mother, instead of supporting or lifting up her daughter, is, in fact, pulling her down.

Ann goes to see her mother's psychiatrist. Adele has fallen in love with him and has created the delusional fantasy that he will marry her. The psychiatrist tells Ann, "'Try not to depend on your mother very much. She's not responsible enough to take care of herself, not to mention another person.'" Ann tells him, "'I don't know what to do. . . . I mean, I lie sometimes, too. I lie to people I'll never see again, and my friends, they don't really know me.'" It is significant that, for the first time, Ann has confided in an adult who is not her mother. She is aware of the line between fact and fantasy, which her mother cannot seem to locate or fathom.

Another significant act of separation and transformation on Ann's part occurs when she cuts her long hair. It is apparent that Ann has become more independent from Adele in the way she tells her about the cut: "'I'm just telling you. For your *information*. I'm not asking for advice. I'm just saying.'" Her mother comes with her to the appointment but at the same time cannot bear to witness Ann cutting her beautiful hair. "'You'll just let anyone be your mother, won't you? You let anyone but me.'" (448) Ann is attempting to forge her own identity and direction, to prepare herself for an adulthood her own mother has not fully entered or accepted.

The Search for a Home

Throughout *Anywhere but Here*, Ann makes repeated references to her grandparents' land in Wisconsin, where they built their house years ago. She lived there at one point as well, and it is the only place that she thinks of as being a home:

> Once, a long time ago, we had a home, too. It was a plain white house in the country. . . .
> I spent time outside, hidden, trying to talk to the trees. It seemed then that the land around our house was more than owned, it was the particular place we were meant to be. Sometimes I thought I would stay there forever, that all the sounds of the yard would teach us about the world. But the trees never answered.
> My mother had been born there, on an old kitchen table, but she saw it as an ordinary house on a dusty dead-end road off the highway. . . . She thought it was chance, bad luck that brought us here. She always meant to move.

For Ann, her grandparents' house is where she feels the most rooted, and the pull of family and roots, which drives her mother away, draws Ann all the more strongly.

When Ann leaves her mother in California to go east for college, she does not return to visit for many years, despite traveling to see her aunt and extended family in Wisconsin. "My thin grandfather and my grandmother, my own mother and Carol had walked exactly here, secrets in their hearts, opening the mailbox door. . . . People we wouldn't recognize, strangers, would touch the land after us, pack down the same earth, without ever knowing how beautiful we found it, how troubling."

When Ann finally goes to California to visit her mother, she finds her living in a nice house on the beach in Malibu. At first, she thinks that Adele has possibly changed her ways and is impressed with her mother's new, clean house and life. "She must have always wanted to live like this; from one perfect outfit to the next, nothing in between, every day crisp new clothes, nothing to be ashamed of, ever, anywhere. She always loved new things. Someone could always be watching." In truth, her mother has not bought the house. Though everything looks perfect, when Adele tries to make a special meal, the food tastes horrible. Once again, appearances—rather than the underlying reality—are what count most in Adele's world. Ann's journey away from her mother's negative influence is a movement toward reality, maturity, and self-acceptance.

KHALED HOSSEINI

Biography

KHALED HOSSEINI was born in 1965 in Kabul, Afghanistan, where his father worked for the Afghan Foreign Ministry. In 1970, Hosseini's family moved to Iran, where his father worked for the Afghan embassy for three years, before returning to Afghanistan. In 1976, the family moved to Paris, France, where they remained during the coup of the People's Democratic Party of Afghanistan in 1978 and subsequent Soviet invasion. They sought political asylum in the United States in 1980, relocating to San Jose, California.

Hosseini graduated high school in San Jose and went on to study biology at Santa Clara University. He then entered the medical school at University of California at Davis, earning his M.D. in 1993. He began writing his first novel in 2001, while also practicing medicine.

As a child, Hosseini read mostly Persian poetry, as well as many Persian translations of Western literature. His memory of childhood in pre-Soviet Afghanistan is a fond one, and he often borrows from these early memories in his writing.

His first novel, *The Kite Runner*, was published in 2003, and has since become an international best-seller, with more than 10 million copies sold worldwide. *The Kite Runner* was adapted into a film of the same name in 2007. His second book, *A Thousand Splendid Suns*, was published in 2007. The previous year, Hosseini was named goodwill envoy to the United Nations Refugee Agency.

The Kite Runner

Summary and Analysis

The Kite Runner tells the story of Amir, the son of a rug exporter, spanning his life from his childhood in Afghanistan to his adult years in California as a political refugee. The story of Amir runs parallel to the story of Hassan, Amir's childhood servant and best friend, until their lives are ruptured, first by a tragic personal event, then by the political events of their country.

The novel covers a time period spanning from the 1960s to 2001. During those more than four decades, Afghanistan underwent numerous changes, the relatively peaceful monarchy falling to a nonviolent coup in 1973, followed by the Soviet invasion in 1978, and later the reign of the Taliban, which ended with the American invasion after the terrorist attacks on September 11, 2001. It is against this political backdrop that the lives of Amir and Hassan unfold. Amir is the son of a wealthy merchant and is Pashtun, the largest ethnic group in Afghanistan. Hassan is born the son of the family's servant, hence his servant, and a Hazara, a Persian-speaking Afghan minority group. For centuries, the Pashtuns had persecuted the Hazaras, in part because of their ethnic and religious differences: Pashtuns were Sunni Muslims, whereas Hazaras identified with the Shi'a branch of the religion.

In the beginning of the novel, Amir and Hassan are best friends who do everything together, despite their differing social status. Then, in 1975, when Amir is twelve years old, a tragic event occurs in the lives of the two boys. During a kite-flying competition, in which Hassan is "running" or chasing after the losing kite so that Amir may win, Hassan is brutally attacked and raped by a sadistic young man named Assef. Amir witnesses the attack from behind a wall and does nothing to stop it, eventually running away in fear. This single event comes to haunt him for years to come, and the guilt he feels over his inaction and subsequent cruel treatment of Hassan tortures him all the more.

Several years later, Afghanistan is once again in the midst of political upheaval. First a coup overturns the monarchy, ushering in Aghanistan's first president. Then several years later, the Soviets invade. Amir and his father escape to Pakistan then seek asylum in the United States. They leave everything behind and start anew in Fremont, California. Despite this physical escape and relocation, Amir still carries the guilt about his friend's sexual assault with him to his adopted country. Eventually, Amir meets a beautiful Afghan woman and has his father ask for her hand in marriage. Shortly after their wedding, his father dies of cancer. It is only years later, when Amir gets a phone call from his father's friend Rahin Khan, that the past returns, and Amir goes back to Afghanistan to confront and address his unresolved feelings. By this time, the country was under the restrictive control and violent regime of the Taliban, and Amir has to risk his life to make amends.

Major Themes

The Inescapable Past

Two aspects or versions of the past—the political and the personal past—interweave in *The Kite Runner*. The book opens with the narrator, Amir, looking back on this conflicted past with an awareness of the ways defining events in the past cannot be altered: "I became what I am today at the age of twelve, on a frigid over-cast day in the winter of 1975. . . . That was a long time ago, but it's wrong what they say about the past, I've learned, about how you can bury it. Because the past claws its way out." With this cryptic opening, before it is revealed what occurred on this day, we learn the central theme of the book: The past is inescapable.

The past as a series of events—which, taken together, form a history—comes up again and again to haunt the main character. History is unfolding throughout the book, in Afghanistan and in the United States, and the effects are felt in both large and small ways—affecting entire nations and touching the lives of two boys. Amir and Hassan are as close as two friends can be; they play together, they live on the same land, they know everything about each other. The gaps or distance that remains between them, however, are also large, as Amir points out: "Because history isn't easy to overcome. Neither is religion. In the end, I was a Pashtun and he was a Hazara, I was Sunni and he was Shi'a, and nothing was ever going to change that. Nothing."

Two different time frames inform and affect Amir's narration, creating a con-trast between the before and after. The relative calm that prevailed in Afghanistan, before the times of upheaval, violence, and war, is mirrored in the innocence of the two boys before they are afflicted by cruelty and violence. When Amir first hears gunshots in the streets, he notes, "They were foreign sounds to us then. The generation of Afghan children whose ears would know nothing but the sounds of bombs and gunfire was not yet born . . . none of us had any notion that a way of life had ended." The gunfire marks the end of an era and of a particular way of life in Afghanistan: "If not quite yet, then at least it was the beginning of the end. The end, the official end, would come first in April 1978 with the communist coup d'etat, and then in December 1979, when Russian tanks would roll into the very same streets where Hassan and I played, bringing the death of the Afghanistan I knew and marking the start of a still ongoing era of bloodletting." Such a major historical transition occurs rapidly: "Kabul awoke the next morning to find that the monarchy was a thing of the past. The king, Kahir Shah, was away in Italy. In his absence, his cousin Daoud Khan had ended the king's forty-year reign with a bloodless coup." The way of life that Amir has known in his home country has ended. This shift in reality and loss of innocence foreshadow the personal rift that occurs between Amir and Hassan.

The Father-Son Relationship

Another recurring theme in *The Kite Runner* is the importance of familial ties, most significantly the father-son relationship. Amir's relationship with his father, whom he calls Baba (Persian for "papa"), changes over time, especially when the pair immigrates to the United States. In Afghanistan, Amir's father is a more dom-inating figure, whose approval Amir seeks, while this desire to receive his father's admiration causes him resentment and anger. "With me as his glaring exception, my father molded the world around him to his liking. The problem, of course, was that Baba saw the world in black and white. And he got to decide what was black and what was white. You can't love a person like that without fearing him too. Maybe even hating him a little." Baba's apparent disapproval of his son may be directly linked to the fact that his wife died while giving birth to Amir: "[T]he truth of it was, I always felt that Baba hated me a little. And why not? After all, I had killed his beloved wife, his beautiful princess, hadn't I? The least I could have done was to have had the decency to have turned out a little more like him."

Amir's desire for his father's approval is mixed with jealousy toward Hassan, who also received his share of Baba's attention. If Baba bought Amir a kite, he would buy one for Hassan as well. "If I changed my mind and asked for a bigger and fancier kite, Baba would buy it for me—but then he'd buy it for Hassan too. Sometimes I wished he wouldn't do that. Wished he'd let me be the favorite." The rivalry between the boys is later revealed to be somewhat justified: The two are, in fact, half brothers and have been raised almost as siblings, sharing the same wet nurse as infants. As Ali, Hassan's father, observes, "there was a brotherhood between people who had fed from the same breast, a kinship that not even time could break."

For Amir, one of the most troubling aspects of getting his father's attention and approval is that the thing that Amir does best—write stories—does not impress his father. When Amir tries to get his father to read one of his stories, the kind family friend Rahim Khan reads it instead and gives Amir the praise and approval he so desperately wants from his father.

The Loss of Childhood Innocence

As the novel's title indicates, kites are a common image in the book. They emerge as a symbol of temporary freedom, the ability to briefly transcend life and all earthbound realities. Kite flying is a winter activity in Kabul: "[A]s the trees froze and ice sheathed the roads, the chill between Baba and me thawed a little. And the reason for that was the kites. Baba and I lived in the same house, but in different spheres of existence. Kites were the one paper-thin slice of intersection between those spheres." Kite flying, thus, exists in the novel as more than a mere entertainment or activity. It also helps to drive the plot and unify the novel's narrative. It is the kite-flying competition that brings about the central conflict that divides the young friends. Kite flying factors into the end of the novel as well, finally bringing a degree of resolution to the story.

Amir wants to win the kite-flying competition to prove his worth to his father: "I was going to win, and I was going to run that last kite. Then I'd bring it home and show it to Baba. Show him once and for all that his son was worthy. Then maybe my life as a ghost in this house would finally be over . . . and maybe, just maybe, I would finally be pardoned for killing my mother." Amir and Hassan are partners in the competition. Amir flies the kites and "cuts" the strings of his competitors' kites with his own string, which is studded with glued-on shards of glass, while Hassan runs to catch the fallen kites that Amir has grounded. It is a two-part process, and as Amir explains, there are no real rules: "Afghans are an independent people. Afghans cherish customs but abhor rules. And so it was with kite fighting. The rules were simple: No rules. Fly your kite. Cut your opponent. Good luck." Hassan also possesses an innate or second sense for kite-running. "Over the years, I had seen a lot of guys run kites. But Hassan was by far the greatest kite runner I'd ever seen. It was downright eerie the way he always got to the spot the kite would land *before* the kite did, as if he had some sort of inner compass."

Throughout the competition, Amir keeps thinking of his father: "I kept stealing glances at Baba sitting with Rahim Khan on the roof, wondered what he was thinking. Was he cheering for me? Or did a part of him enjoy watching me fail? That was the thing about kite flying: Your mind drifted with the kite." In the end, Amir wins and finally experiences his father's unqualified approval. When he sees his father celebrating his win, "that right there was the single greatest moment of my twelve years of life, seeing Baba on that roof, proud of me at last."

Unfortunately, Amir's euphoria is short lived. Hassan has to fetch the losing kite for the victory to be official. When a local bully Assef demands the kite and Hassan refuses to give it up, Assef beats and rapes the boy. While looking for Hassan, Amir witnesses the attack, paralyzed with fear and unable to stop it or seek help for his friend. Amir and Hassan never tell anyone what happened, much less discuss the violent incident themselves. When Amir comes home, he is finally praised by Baba for winning the tournament, but Amir realizes that the opposite would have been the case if Baba had known what had happened.

Violence and Trauma

Amir's victory is soured by the shocking event he witnesses in the competition's aftermath. Born to a German mother and an Afghan father, Assef has a "well-earned reputation for savagery." As Amir recounts, "Years later, I learned an English word for the creature that Assef was, a word for which a good Farsi equivalent does not exist: 'sociopath.'" Assef is both violent and racist—looking at Hassan, he says, "Afghanistan is the land of Pashtuns. It always has been, always will be. We are the true Afghans, the pure Afghans, not this Flat-Nose here. His people pollute our homeland, our watan. They dirty our blood."

Amir makes a halfhearted attempt to tell someone about the trauma of the event: "'I watched Hassan get raped,' I said to no one. Baba stirred in his sleep. . . . A part of me was hoping someone would wake up and hear, so I wouldn't have to live with this lie anymore. But no one woke up and in the silence that followed, I understood the nature of my new curse: I was going to get away with it. . . . That was the night I became an insomniac." From this point on, Amir's guilt grown too immense, he avoids the boy who had once been his closest friend: "Hassan milled about the periphery of my life after that. I made sure our paths crossed as little as possible, planned my day that way. Because when he was around, the oxygen seeped out of the room. My chest tightened and I couldn't draw enough air." When Amir suggests that they get new servants, his father reacts angrily: "'Hassan's not going anywhere. . . . He's staying right here with us, where he belongs. This is his home and we're his family. Don't you ever ask me that question again!'" Years later, Amir is finally told the truth of the situation: Hassan is a blood relation, the product of an affair between Baba and his servant's wife. The information comes too late, however, as despite his father's protestations, Amir eventually manages to drive Hassan and his father away, thus destroying the family circle. Shortly afterward, the country descends into violence, and Amir and his father flee to the United States.

Finding a Safe Haven

Amir's relationship with his father changes when they go to the United States. His father is no longer a wealthy man of status but is instead a poor immigrant working at a service station. Amir is the one who takes care of his father, rather than being under his father's command, and he chooses his own path of becoming a writer.

The United States is presented as a way out for Amir—both as a refuge from the political strife of Afghanistan as well as an escape from the memory of Hassan. The vastness of the new country makes it all the more of an escape—"beyond every freeway lay another freeway, beyond every city another city, hills beyond mountains and mountains beyond hills, and, beyond those, more cities and more people." Most of all, Amir's new land exists to him as a release, no matter how temporary, from the power of memory, guilt, and responsibility:

> Long before the Roussi army marched into Afghanistan, long before villages were burned and schools destroyed, long before mines were planted like seeds of death and children buried in rock-piled graves, Kabul had become a city of ghosts for me. A city of harelipped ghosts.
>
> America was different. America was a river, roaring along, unmindful of the past. I could wade into this river, let my sins drown to the bottom, let the waters carry me someplace far. Someplace with no ghosts, no memories, and no sins.

Although Amir finds a new life in the United States and eventually falls in love and marries, he still cannot entirely escape his past. When he asks the young Afghan woman Soraya to marry him, she confesses her own past secrets to him and asks him if he still wants to marry her because of it. "I envied her. Her secret was out. Spoken. Dealt with. I opened my mouth and almost told her how I'd betrayed Hassan, lied, driven him out, and destroyed a forty-year relationship between Baba and Ali. But I didn't."

A Return to Origins

After Amir's father dies, he receives a call from Rahim Khan telling Amir to come to see him in Pakistan: "*Come. There is a way to be good again.*" (192) Amir finds Rahim in a small apartment in Peshawar, emaciated and with only a few months to live. After much talk about the political situation, Rahim Khan reveals why he asked Amir to come see him: to tell Amir the truth about Hassan. After Amir and his father fled, Rahim Khan was living in their house and eventually asked Hassan and his wife to come and live with him. The couple had a son, Sohrab, who became an orphan when Hassan and his wife were killed by the Taliban. Rahim Khan also reveals the long-held family secret that Hassan is Amir's half-brother. Rahim Khan's dying wish to Amir is to go to Afghanistan, find Sohrab, and bring him back.

Amir is finally presented with the opportunity to redeem himself: "What Rahim Khan revealed to me changed things. Made me see how my entire life, long before the winter of 1975, dating back to when that singing Hazara woman was still nursing me, had been a cycle of lies, betrayals, and secrets. *There is a way to be good again*, he'd said. A way to end the cycle. With a little boy. An orphan. Hassan's son. Somewhere in Kabul."

After crossing the Khyber Pass and entering Afghanistan, Amir feels like a "tourist in my own country," and his driver tells him, "That's the real Afghanistan. . . . You've *always* been a tourist here, you just didn't know it." As Baba once told Amir about the religious mullahs, "They do nothing but thumb their prayer beads and recite a book written in a tongue they don't even understand. . . . God help us all if Afghanistan ever falls into their hands." Now, Baba's greatest fear has come to pass, and the country is run by the Islamic fundamentalists who make up the Taliban.

Redemption

In *The Kite Runner*, the violence and sadism of the Taliban is epitomized in the character of Assef. When Amir finally locates Hassan's son, he has been taken from the orphanage by the Taliban and is being abused and tortured by Assef, Hassan's childhood rapist. Assef is a brutal sadist who justifies his violence with the religious doctrines of the Taliban. Amir goes to see him and has to endure his description of the Taliban's door-to-door killing of Hazara civilians in Mazar in 1998: "'You don't know the meaning of the word "liberating" until you've done that, stood in a roomful of targets, let the bullets fly, free of guilt and remorse, knowing you are virtuous, good, and decent. Knowing you're doing God's work. It's breathtaking.'"

Assef remembers Amir from their childhood in Kabul. He decides to fight Amir and release him afterward only if he survives the beating. Amir nearly dies during the fight, but he is finally freed from his lifelong guilt:

> I don't know at what point I started laughing, but I did. It hurt to laugh, hurt my jaws, my ribs, my throat . . . the harder I laughed, the harder he

kicked me, punched me, scratched me. "WHAT'S SO FUNNY?" Assef kept roaring with each blow.... What was so funny was that, for the first time since the winter of 1975, I felt at peace.... My body was broken—just how badly I wouldn't find out until later—but I felt healed. Healed at last. I laughed.

In the end, Amir escapes with his life and Hassan's son, his conscience finally wiped clean by the trials he undergoes in his native country on behalf of Hassan and his family.

Amir returns to the United States with Sohrab, who is scarred and traumatized by the violence and abuse that have marked his young life. When they first arrive, Sohrab does not speak. The novel's final scene mirrors the beginning, in which Amir and Hassan are flying kites, their innocence still intact and uncompromised. Now, Amir is flying a kite with Hassan's son, and he finds hope in Sohrab's smile. Amir can now remember Hassan through his son, who emerges as a vital connection to the homeland Amir has left behind: "I heard a crow cawing somewhere and I looked up. The park shimmered with snow so fresh, so dazzling white, it burned my eyes.... I smelled turnip *qurma* now. Dried mulberries. Sour oranges. Sawdust and walnuts.... Then far away, across the stillness, a voice calling us home, the voice of a man who dragged his right leg." Despite the losses that have touched the characters' lives, Hosseini is able to summon a hopeful note in the connection and reconciliation that conclude his novel.

CLAIRE MESSUD

Biography

CLAIRE MESSUD was born in Connecticut in 1966, to a Canadian mother and a French-Algerian father. She grew up in Canada and Australia before returning to the United States as a teenager. Her debut novel, *When the World Was Steady* (1995), was nominated for the PEN/Faulkner Award. In 1999, she published her second book, *The Last Life*, about three generations of a French-Algerian family. Her 2001 work, *The Hunters*, consists of two novellas. Her most recent novel, *The Emperor's Children*, was written while she was a fellow at the Radcliffe Institute for Advanced Study in 2004–2005. The American Academy of Arts and Letters has recognized Messud's talent with both an Addison Metcalf Award and a Strauss Living Award. Messud has also been awarded a Guggenheim Fellowship.

Messud is married to the British literary critic James Wood. They live in Washington, D.C., and Somerville, Massachusetts, with their two children.

The Emperor's Children

Summary and Analysis

The Emperor's Children takes place over a nine-month period, from March to November 2001. The story unfolds in the time leading up to and following the World Trade Center attacks on September 11, 2001. Rather than focusing on the political implications of that time in American history, the novel instead turns its attention to a handful of people whose lives intersect in the backdrop of literary New York. Three friends from college, on the cusp of thirty and trying to make their way in Manhattan, run up against disillusionment and cynicism and try to succeed, both personally and professionally, in uncertain times.

Danielle Minkoff is a documentary television journalist and producer. When the book opens, she is in Australia conducting research for a possible story. Within the first few pages, it is clear where her true home is:

> She was a New Yorker. There was, for Danielle Minkoff, only New York. Her work was there, her friends were there—even her remote acquaintances from college at Brown ten years ago were there—and she had made her home in the cacophonous, cozy comfort of the Village. From her studio . . . she surveyed lower Manhattan like a captain at the prow of her ship.

Danielle, being a documentary producer, is in many ways the book's central character. She is the moral center, a clear-eyed presence able to see through artifice and distortion. "Reality, or rather facing it, was Danielle's great credo; although if she were wholly honest, here and now, she believed a little in magic, too."

Danielle is the best friend of Marina Thwaite, the beautiful daughter of the famous Murray Thwaite, a journalist and writer who is well known in the literary and intellectual circles of Manhattan. When the novel opens, Marina is facing a crisis. She has broken up with her boyfriend and moved back in with her parents on the Upper West Side. Soon to be thirty years old, she has also started receiving an allowance from them. In addition, she is desperately trying to finish a book—about children's fashions and their cultural implications—for which she is years late in meeting the contracted due date. In many ways, the success and advantages she has realized are attributable to her beauty and the fact that she is the daughter of a literary celebrity. As Danielle says of her friend, "'Sometimes I just want to say to her, what if you walked into a room, Marina, and nobody stopped talking, and nobody turned around? What if nobody offered to cut your hair for free or to carry your luggage? What then?'"

Julius Clarke is Danielle and Marina's other close friend from college. He is a smart, acerbic writer and critic who has reinvented his identity after leaving his small hometown in Michigan. His primary anxiety is that his accomplishments

> were few, and fading . . . throughout his twenties, he lived a life of Wildean excess and insouciance that seemed an accomplishment in itself, the contemporary example of the enfant terrible. . . . He was aware that at thirty he stretched the limits of the charming wastrel, that some actual sustained endeavor might be in order were he not to fade, wisplike, away: from charming wastrel to needy, boring failure was but a few, too few, short steps.

Julius, more than Danielle or Marina, is most interested in power and ambition.

Orbiting this circle of three friends, several other characters help to frame the narrative: Murray Thwaite, Marina's father; Frederick "Bootie" Tubb, Murray's nephew from upstate New York; and Ludovic Seeley, a brilliant and arrogant Australian magazine publisher on whom Danielle has developed a crush.

Bootie is a smart, promising 19-year-old who has dropped out of college, to his mother's dissappointment, and is looking to learn from his Uncle Murray the "truth" rather than what he would be taught in a classroom. His revelation, which comes to him while enrolled at college "with a visceral force, [was] 'This is a farce. I am living, we are all living, a complete farce . . . ' The Land of Lies in which most people were apparently content to live—in which you paid money to an institution and went out nightly to get drunk instead of reading the books . . . and then you declared yourself *educated*—was not sufficient for Bootie. . . . So Bootie had called an end to the farce." In many ways, Bootie functions as the voice of truth in the novel, and he hopes that by moving to New York City, from his small, upstate New York town, he will finally be able to access the truth that he seeks. His father having died, Murray is the mentor Bootie craves; he wanted "to be granted access to their mysterious world. His uncle was, without question, a great man; and Bootie would try to be worthy of him." Messud writes:

> Bootie believed that his uncle and his family was his "only hope, his ticket out." His uncle was a man who had chosen the path of the mind, who had opted for integrity over glory, even if it had brought him fame rather than the obscurity advocated by Emerson. . . . Bootie thought of how to present himself to Murray Thwaite—as a kind of disciple, an independent follower.

Bootie was, "he decided, like a pilgrim in the old days, a pilgrim in search of knowledge."

Major Themes

Identity

Throughout *The Emperor's Children*, Messud weaves in several recurring themes. One is the question of identity, particularly in the case of becoming an adult. Over the course of the novel, the characters are often portrayed as playing roles or trying to "become" something. One traditional literary genre is the bildungsroman, a narrative that traces a protagonist's maturation or coming of age. Messud employs this universal theme of growth and self-discovery as it plays out in the lives of her precocious and privileged characters. They are making the transition from their twenties, in which the world seems more open and their lives more unfettered and free, into their thirties, in which there is more pressure to have "arrived," to have a more definitive sense of identity and direction, if not a list of accomplishments to match. In the especially competitive, often elitist world of Manhattan that Messud's characters inhabit, this proves to be a difficult process for the three friends.

The Emperor's Clothes

Murray Thwaite is the "emperor" of the title, in the sense that he is the older, more accomplished character. He has built his life into something of a myth. The chapter titled "'Introducing Murray Thwaite' by Roanne Levine (newspaper staff)"—which consists of a college newspaper article written by a young admirer—serves to uphold the myth:

> Few contemporary journalists are as versatile, as erudite, and as controversial as Murray Thwaite.... He is a dynamic speaker, and unafraid of the most challenging questions.... Mr. Thwaite has one daughter, Marina...."I never told my daughter to become a writer," he said. "Quite the opposite. I figure, if you can do something else, do. Because it's a stimulating life, but an uncertain one. I did bring her up though to understand that integrity is everything, it's all you've got. And that if you have a voice, a gift, you're morally bound to exploit it."

The distortion contained in the article—in which Murray Thwaite appears authentic and sincere and his close relationship with his daughter is prominently on display— only serves to confirm his inflated ego and exaggerated sense of self-importance. It is in the shadow of this towering and overwhelming presence that Marina struggles to define herself. Talking with her father at home, in the "inner sanctum" of his office, she laments the fact that "when you were thirty you were already famous":

> Murray Thwaite had little patience for this. He suddenly saw his daughter as a monster he and [his wife] had created—they and a society of excess....
> What, he wondered, should follow? "But the question is, what do you want to do with your life?"
> "I want—you know, what I've always wanted, Daddy. To do something important."
> Could she not hear herself? Even that student at Columbia—even she had surely not been so naïve, and ten years younger, too.

It is telling that Marina's desire to do something "important" is linked to or revolves around the idea of being famous. This notion seems to run counter to the noble assertion that the talented have a moral obligation to develop their gift for its own sake and not for acquiring notoriety or fame. Murray's identification of New York as a "society of excess" is a recurring motif in the book, one that Messud subtly links to the historical reality of the terrorist attacks that occur midway through the narrative.

This atmosphere of excess and distortion influences the lives of the characters and is reflected in how they are portrayed. Ludovic Seeley emerges as the person determined to unmask Murray Thwaite. Ludovic comes to New York to start a new magazine that he hopes will expose and counteract the falsehood and hollowness that he sees in intellectuals such as Thwaite. As he tells Danielle:

> What could be rarer, more precious, more compelling than unmasking these hacks for what they are? Than an instrument to trumpet that the emperor has no clothes. . . . Show people that Murray Thwaite is the Wizard of Oz, a tiny, pointless man roaring behind a curtain. Then learn what they are, and show themselves.

Ludovic seduces Marina and eventually convinces her what her unfinished book is actually about. To be titled *The Emperor's Children Have No Clothes*, he explains to her what this means: "As parents, we visit our complexes, whatever they may be, upon our children—our neuroses, our hopes and fears, our discontents. Just the way our broader society is like a parent, and visits its complexes upon the citizenry, if you will . . ."

He goes on to speak as if he is writing a review of the book, laying the groundwork for a father-daughter split:

> Marina Thwaite's groundbreaking book demystifies these complexes . . . [and] reveals the forms and patterns that both are and lie beneath the fabric of our society [baring] children, their parents, and our culture at large to an unprecedented and frank scrutiny, and in her truth-telling, shows us incontrovertibly that the emperor's children have no clothes.

In effect, Marina is simply exchanging one father figure for another in coming to accept Ludovic's way of seeing the world she inhabits. Her father and Ludovic, her future husband, are essentially the same character, however, and she remains in the childish position of following a dominant male.

Distortion and Disillusionment

In the course of working for his uncle, Bootie increasingly becomes disillusioned with him. Bootie's view of his powerful relative undergoes a significant change: "[T]hings looked different; Murray looked different: still an imposing façade, to be sure; but a hollow monument." Bootie discovers that Murray has plagiarized himself, publishing the same comment worded the same way twice. His uncle dismisses the charge casually when Bootie asks him about it.

> But later, [Bootie] realized, it stayed with him. He went back to Emerson, whom he felt understood these things. "All persons exist to society by some shining trait of beauty or utility which they have. We borrow the proportions of the man from that one fine feature, and finish the portrait symmetrically; which is false, for the rest of this body is small

or deformed." It was a disappointment, a deformation, albeit minor. His
uncle was perhaps a little lazy, a little lax. He could forgive it, but he
wouldn't forget.

Bootie had also come across his uncle's secret unfinished book project, which Bootie had read in "fervent snatches" and found to be "both pretentious and trite. . . .
He believed now that the Great Man had been an illusion all along, mere window
dressing. Reluctantly, he slid into alignment with Ludovic Seeley: Murray Thwaite
was one great con trick, a lazy, self-absorbed con trick." To add to his growing disillusionment with his uncle, Bootie also discovers that Murray is having an affair
with Marina's friend Danielle. In an act of defiance, Bootie decides to write a piece
for Ludovic's magazine that will expose Murray and "tell the truth, show the world
the man as he was."

For Bootie, the issue becomes a question of honesty: Murray was presenting
an image or way of being to the world that was not true to his actual character:

> Murray Thwaite claimed that honesty was paramount; but the word had,
> for him, only his own meaning. He claimed that he fought injustice, that
> his life had been devoted to what he deemed a "moral journalism." He
> claimed that he lived for and by his independence, his own wits. He pre-
> sumed to opine on paper about how life should be led, about the very
> meaning of the word, when he was evidently—Bootie meant this in all se-
> riousness: Bootie had *evidence*—someone for whom words had no fixed
> meaning. Somebody needed to make this clear, and public.

Bootie, as a seeker of truth, is driven to speak clearly and reasonably about the artifice and falseness he sees around him. He feels it is his duty to tell the truth about
Murray and thereby expose him as being a lazy, pretentious, and hollow man.

Language and the Power of Words

Messud's novel, with its writers, publishers, and journalists, centers on language
and words, their power and ability to distort and misrepresent. When Murray
finally gets around to reading Marina's book, he is disappointed, finding it to be
"trite garbage, introductory sociology garbarge. . . . The book as a whole struck
him as an artfully wrapped gift box, a flurry of elegant paper and ribbons that,
when opened proved to be empty." He meets her for lunch to tell her that he thinks
she should not publish the book, that it has no reason for being: "Call me old fashioned, but in my world a book—if only on account of the trees chopped down to
produce it; but for many other reasons as well—should justify its existence. It must
have a *raison d'être* [reason for being]. I just don't see one here. I'm sorry."

Ironically, this same harsh bit of fatherly advice that Murray gives is then extended
or offered to Murray in Bootie's article. Bootie sends copies of his piece to both Murray

and Marina, and is quickly ousted from the family. Left to his own devices, he moves to a rental in Brooklyn, and is thus exiled from Manhattan. He moves "off the radar."

Setting and Historical Context

The importance of setting is another recurring element in *The Emperor's Children*, as New York City emerges as both a real place (subject to unexpected and violent attacks) and a fantastical notion or abstract ideal. Murray's notion of excess shapes and colors Messud's portrayal of her novel's setting. Linked to this material and intellectual excess is the sense of entitlement many of the characters possess: "[I]t seems as though entitlement, that mysterious gift, explains everything everyone does these days."

Danielle is enveloped in the city. She sees it from her apartment and her roof, and has a vision of its overarching pattern:

> Danielle was struck again by the glory of the city around them, its glittering stalagmites and arterial avenues, strung with the beaded headlights of the ever-starting, ever-stopping traffic. Even the dark patches, the flat rooftops of the brick and brownstone buildings to the immediate south and west, or the hollow she knew to be a playground by day—even these ellipses were vital to the pattern. Farther downtown, a cluster of skyscrapers rose, alight, into the night, stolid mercantile reassurance in the mad whimsy of the city.

Danielle emerges as the embodiment of the city, as she comes to serve a function in the narrative similar to the city's role: She sees the other characters "as if she were the audience and they players upon the stage, [with] this peculiar sense of clear vision."

Messud introduces, as the background to this world of excess and indulgence, the historical reality of the 2001 terrorist attacks. Danielle takes an illicit helicopter ride with Murray on the evening before September 11, and she is like a child being shown the city, flown "over the glinting river, around the vast buildings upon which the shadow of night was beginning to fall, down, out in an arc to winking Lady Liberty and back around the island's tip." This romantic vision of the nighttime city stands in stark contrast to the violence and chaos that would prevail the following day. Such a grim and sobering intrusion of reality similarly contrasts the characters' lives of indulgence and wish fulfillment.

The Effects of Violence and Tragedy

Danielle and Murray wake up in her apartment on September 11; it is the first time he has deliberately lied to his wife and not spent the night with her. Murray cries out when he sees the smoking building, and they see everything unfold "in stereo, watching through the window—their view spectacularly, hideously unimpeded—and watching on the screen . . . and everything they saw seemed somehow more and less real on the television because what they saw with their own eyes they couldn't quite believe." Murray leaves Danielle to walk uptown to his wife, and Danielle is left alone, numb and devastated, by both the larger event and the smaller romantic abandonment.

The novel's most honest—and selfish—reaction to the day perhaps comes from Ludovic, who feels that his magazine, about to launch, is now finished. "They're all dead. Of course they're all dead," he tells Marina of the individuals pictured on the missing person posters in Union Square. "It's the land of lies here, isn't it? So nobody's going to say that. And we're not going to say it, because we don't have a magazine . . . don't kid yourself. The bubble's burst, now. It's over."

In the aftermath of the attacks, Bootie turns out to be missing. On that morning, when he came out of the subway, headed to his temporary job near the towers, and saw the chaos, he simply kept walking, musing as he walked: "this, the end of the world as he knew it, changed everything. The Tower of Babel tumbling. An end to false idols. And Murray . . . who was emperor in this place of pretense—surely even Murray, above all Murray, would be toppled by this." Bootie feels freed by the event and embraces a new credo of "mutability, precisely the capacity to spin like an atom, untethered, this thrill of absolute unknownness was not something to be feared. It was the point of it all. To be unrelated. Without context. To be truly and in every way self-reliant. At last." Bootie spends the night in Central Park, then eventually, when Port Authority reopens, takes a bus to Miami, leaving no trace.

Murray, however, is not toppled by the events. He emerges even stronger and more revered than before, his exposure increasing as he writes and speaks about the historical and foreign policy implications of the attacks. When it is erroneously revealed that he lost his only nephew in the attacks, he is considered to have an "immovable integrity": "Murray couldn't help but be aware of the irony that Bootie's death had granted him greater nobility, an importance—he knew it to be false—as a man of justice, unswayed by the arrows of misfortune. But perhaps, had he been able to see it, Bootie would at last have been proud of his uncle." Using the tragedy to bolster his public image, Murray realizes it comes at the expense of his own sense of integrity.

Coming of Age

At the end of the novel, each of the three main characters has undergone a significant transformation in a relatively short time. The reality of the terrorist attacks seems to usher in a forced or startlingly new awareness, and Messud's young strivers are compelled to embrace a new model or mode of their adulthood. Julius, his face scarred after his jealous lover attacks him, realizes that his altered appearance similarly starts to change others' perception of him. Though he wants to remain the same, he is forced to revise his notion of himself:

> You don't think of yourself as scarred. You forget. And you think you can just keep being your same self. But everyone sees you, they see a changed

person, and the ones who know the story see you as changed in a very particular way, which isn't so nice. And then they remind you, over and over again, and then, I think, eventually you get changed, from the outside in, you have to absorb it, somehow.

Marina, for her part, finds that married life is not all she thought it would be, as she starts to notice the unpleasantness that settles in the place of seduction: "he'd snapped harshly at her . . . his tone had been different, a new tone, exasperated, that she'd not heard before, or not heard directed at *her* before, that was for sure, and now she was wondering was *this* what it meant to be married?"

After the attacks on the city, Danielle notices that life has more of a weight and seriousness than it used to:

[G]rowing up, coupling, was a process of growing away from mirth, as if, like an amphibian, one ceased to breathe in the same way. . . . All of them, all three of them: a year ago, they'd still been linked, inexorably and, they'd thought, forever. It was supposedly better this way—each of them had found her heart's desire—but did they laugh as they had done for so many years? Would they ever laugh that way again, or was it over, now, in the Realm of Adult Sobriety?

Heartbroken, depressed, and nearly suicidal, Danielle calls her mother, who brings her to Florida and attempts to nurse her back to health. Danielle realizes, however, that, though she wants her mother to save her, she cannot. Danielle must accept responsibility for herself, must return and live her life as an adult. "She thought maybe [her mother] was right; she thought that maybe she shouldn't go back. But she knew that she would, because she didn't want to go anywhere else, or have anywhere else to go. She knew that her life—her future—was there." She returns to New York City to resume and continue her life, albeit on slightly altered terms.

In *The Emperor's Children*, the historical events of the attacks on the Twin Towers frame the broader question of what it is to become an adult, to grow up and arrive at a more mature perspective. For the characters, there is little choice, as the world that surrounds them has been forcibly changed and will never be exactly the same again. At the same time, Messud tempers her novel with a dose of realism: The characters, though different, at the same time accept the fate of the lives they have chosen and found themselves inhabiting.

MOHJA KAHF

Biography

MOHJA KAHF was born in Damascus, Syria, in 1967. She and her family moved to the United States in 1971, first settling in Utah. Her father earned a Ph.D. in economics at the University of Utah, where her mother completed a B.S. in pharmacology. Kahf eventually studied comparative literature, earning a Ph.D. at Rutgers University. She is now an associate professor of comparative literature and a faculty member of the King Fahd Center for Middle East and Islamic Studies at the University of Arkansas, Fayetteville.

An academic writer as well as poet and novelist, Kahf's first book was an academic study titled *Western Representations of Muslim Women: From Termagant to Odalisque* (1999). She is the author of poetry, creative nonfiction, essays, literary criticism, academic scholarship, short fiction, and most recently a novel, *The Girl in the Tangerine Scarf*. Her first book of poetry, *E-mails from Scheherazad*, was a finalist for the 2004 Paterson Poetry Prize.

As a Muslim feminist, Kahf walks a fine line between Islamic tradition and contemporary feminism. She has been both praised and criticized by her fellow Muslims for her innovative approach to being a practicing, moderate Muslim, while also remaining committed to women's rights. Fellow writer and scholar Lisa Suhair Majaj wrote this about her: "Whatever her genre, Kahf offers articulate, passionate challenges to commonplace perceptions of the Middle East, Muslim women and Arab Americans, striking notes of humor, compassion, outrage and celebration that resonate across the literary register."

E-mails from Scheherazad
Summary and Analysis

In her collection of poems, *E-mails from Scheherazad*, Mohja Kahf addresses the particular aspects of being a Syrian immigrant in a contemporary American context. Her poems speak about gender, religion, and ethnicity in the United States with an unusual degree of humor and candor, at once illuminating her experience to those outside her culture while also speaking directly to an Arab-American community.

Scheherazad is the legendary Persian queen who narrates *One Thousand and One Nights*, a compilation of popular stories that was first written down in the tenth century in Iraq but is found in various forms throughout the Arab world. Scheherazad was a virgin who was kept alive by her gift for storytelling. The king delayed her execution night after night as he eagerly anticipated her conclusion to the previous night's story. In the course of the 1,001 nights, the king eventually falls in love with Scheherazad, and he spares her life by making her his queen.

In the poem "E-mail from Scheherazad," Kahf imagines a contemporary Scheherazad who is divorced and teaching creative writing in New Jersey.

> Hi, babe. It's Scheherazad. I'm back
> For the millennium and living in Hackensack,
> New Jersey. I tell stories for a living.
> You ask if there is a living in that.
>
> You must remember: Where I come from,
> Words are to die for. I saved the virgins
> From beheading by the king, who was killing
> Them to still the beast of doubt in him.

In Kahf's version of a feminist Scheherazad, words are all-powerful, and she is not content to stay with the king. Rather, she has found her own voice and uses it for more than simply saving her own life. Mere love is not enough for her, and as a modern woman she finds a vocation in her talent for language.

> I told a story. He began to listen and I found
> That story led to story. Power unleashed, I wound
> The thread around the pirn of night. A thousand days
> Later, we got divorced. He'd settled down
>
> & wanted a wife & not so much an artist.
> I wanted publication. It was hardest,
> Strangely, on my sister, Dunyazad. She
> Was the one who nightly used to start it.

She and my ex do workshops now in schools
On art & conflict resolution. Narrative rules!
I teach creative writing at Montclair State,
And I'm on my seventh novel and book tour.

Shahrayar and I share custody of our little girl.
We split up amicably. I taught him to heal
His violent streak through stories, after all,
And he helped me uncover my true call.

Kahf uses the motif of Scheherazad to reclaim her role as a strong Arab female character. The portrayal of Scheherazad by Western writers has often been as a passive and submissive sexual object. According to writer Susan Muaddi Darraj,

[T]he voice of the Arab woman had been warped since it first made its way westward. Scheherazade, the heroine of One Thousand and One Nights, had suffered terribly at the hands of translators. Revered in the East as a heroine for distracting the sultan Shahrayar from his murderous rampage with intriguing stories . . . Scheherazade became nothing more than a harem sex kitten. . . . An intelligent woman, schooled in literature, philosophy, and history, reduced to an erotic, shallow, sex-crazed body behind a veil—it happened many times, with many Arab and/or Eastern women, including Cleopatra, Khadijah, and Aisha.

Kahf presents a darker portrayal of Scheherazad in the poem "So You Think You Know Scheherazad." In it, the legendary storyteller is presented as more of a shapeshifter who brings inner demons to life:

So you think you know Scheherazad
So you think she tells you bedtime stories
that will please and soothe,
invents fairy creatures
who will grant you wishes

Scheherazad invents nothing
Scheherazad awakens
the demons under your bed
They were always there
She locks you in with them

In this version, Scheherazad is the force that summons and releases terrors from "within you and within her / And suddenly Scheherazad is nowhere to be found / but the stories she unlocked go on and on—." The power of the story is like an energy that can be unleashed from within, revealing perhaps the best and worst parts of the self:

> this is the power of the telling of a story—
> And suddenly you find yourself
> swimming through the sea to the Reef of Extremity,
> flying to the Valley of All That Is Possible,
> walking barefoot on a blade
> over the Chasm of Flames,
> landing in a field where you wrestle with Iblis,
>
> whose form changes into your lover,
> into Death, into knowledge, into God,
> whose face changes into Scheherazad—
>
> And suddenly you find yourself.

In this case, Scheherazad as the storyteller holds the power over the outcome. She is a force that exists as both creator and critic, her story emerging as a narrative of self-discovery and self-awareness.

Major Themes

Female Body as Battleground

In Kahf's two versions of Scheherazad, she is portrayed as a humanizing force on the king, helping to control or end his violent tendencies, as well as a changeable and potent demon. As a modern woman who lives in two worlds, Kahf herself is a modern-day Scheherazad who uses words as both a sword and a healing balm. In the poem "Hijab Scene #7," Kahf uses language to deflect and vent her frustrations with being an "other" in the United States:

> No, I'm not bald under the scarf
> No, I'm not from that country
> where women can't drive cars
> No, I would not like to defect
> I'm already American
> But thank you for offering
> What else do you need to know
> relevant to my buying insurance,
> opening a bank account,
> reserving a seat on a flight?
> Yes, I speak English

Yes, I carry explosives
They're called words
And if you don't get up
Off your assumptions,
They're going to blow you away

Kahf allows her impatience with the typical Arab stereotypes to come to the fore, and because she is "already American," she is confident enough to know her rights as a citizen. She is speaking from a universal experience of ethnic stereotyping, while also directly confronting the specific aspects of American ignorance in regard to Arab people. With the line "Yes, I carry explosives," Kahf is not afraid to confront directly the darkest fears of a post–September 11 American political landscape.

In another, simpler version of using words to convey a cultural observation, the poem "Hijab #2" is more to the point:

"You people have such restrictive dress for women,"
she said, hobbling away in three-inch heels and panty hose
to finish out another pink-collar temp pool day.

The female body is often a site for debate in Kahf's poetry. She turns the issue of constraint of the female form on its head by pointing out the Western norms of "three-inch heels and panty hose." In the poem "My Body Is Not Your Battleground," she explicitly addresses both American and Arab notions of her female body, which she places at the center of an ideological battleground.

My body is not your battleground
My hair is neither sacred nor cheap,
neither the cause of your disarray
nor the path to your liberation.
My hair will not bring progress and clean water
if it flies unbraided in the breeze
It will not save us from our attackers
if it is wrapped and shielded from the sun.

Standing in the middle, at the intersection of Eastern and Western modes of thinking, Kahf is able to see each side and influence clearly. The conclusion she draws through her poetry is that neither perspective is entirely accurate or helpful to her. Each perspective or set of cultural expectations actually only leads to a distorted or skewed view of the body and the self. In the end, she asks for both sides to withdraw so that she may celebrate her own body without impediment:

My body is not your battleground
Withdraw from the eastern fronts and the western
Withdraw these armaments and this siege
so that I may prepare the earth
for the new age of lilac and clover,
so that I may celebrate this spring
the pageant of beauty with my sweet love.

Family Migration

In many poems, Kahf writes about immigration and what occurs in the transition from one culture to another. In "The Skaff Mother Tells the Story," a Syrian mother must send her sons away to keep them from getting drafted into the Turkish army. The choice between her sons' survival and being separated from their family wears heavily on the speaker: "The wool of my heart is threadbare after the years and wars / And I keep in a bundle the names of my lost boys. / *Survive*, we told them, and sent them unthinkably away." The journey of Kahf's own family from Syria to the United States also figures prominently in the collection. In "The Roc," Kahf provides brief snapshots of her parents, beginning in the streets of Damascus:

Here's my mom and dad leaving
Damascus, the streets they knew,
the familiar shape of food, the daily
boiling and cooling of fresh milk,
the measurement of time by mosque sounds

The rest of the poem contrasts this original familiarity with the newness and uncertainty of being an immigrant:

Here they are crossing the world,
hoisting up all they know like a sail,
landing in Utah
. . . .

Here's my mother studying
the instructions on the coin-
box of a laundry machine,
enrolling us in kindergarten
. . . .

Here's my father staking his life's
savings on one semester in grad school
. . . .

The simple task of doing laundry becomes a challenging undertaking of decoding another language and culture. The immigrants' world becomes full of risk and doubt, in which they must struggle to do the smallest things and take nothing for granted. The last stanza of the poem contains the often tenuous comfort of reconnecting with Syria, in the form of a telephone call:

> Here they are, mom and dad, telephoning
> back home, where the folks gather around
> the transmission as if it came from the moon.

In "My Grandmother Washes Her Feet in the Sink of the Bathroom at Sears," Kahf juxtaposes a vivid image of a sacred Muslim ritual, the washing of feet in preparation for prayer, with the less than sacred setting of a Sears bathroom. The contrast is both humorous and touching in its urgency, "because she has to pray in the store or miss / the mandatory prayer time for Muslims":

> She does it with great poise, balancing
> herself with one plump matronly arm
> against the automated hot-air hand dryer,
> after having removed her support knee-highs
> and laid them aside, folded in thirds,
> and given me her purse and her packages to hold
> so she can accomplish this august ritual
> and get back to the ritual of shopping for housewares.

The elaborate choreography of her grandmother washing her feet, in all its common, everyday detail, is poignant because it reveals a private religious action that is laid bare for all to see—and judge—in the open arena of a public washroom.

> Respectable Sears matrons shake their heads and frown
> as they notice what my grandmother is doing,
> an affront to American porcelain,
> a contamination of American Standards
> by something foreign and unhygienic
> requiring civic action and possible use of disinfectant spray
> They fluster about and flutter their hands and I can see
> a clash of civilizations brewing in the Sears bathroom

In this poem, Kahf is the intermediary standing in the middle of this clash of civilizations. She sees how the non-Muslim American women react to the old woman washing her feet, but she must also be aligned with and translate for her grandmother. "'You can't do that,' one of the women protests, / turning to me, 'Tell her she can't do that.' / 'We wash our feet five times a day,' / my grandmother declares hotly in Arabic. / 'My feet are cleaner than their sink.'" The granddaughter sees all sides of the situation: "Standing between the door and the mirror, I can see / at multiple angles, my grandmother and the other shoppers, / all of them decent and goodhearted women."

In the poem "Cherries," Kahf imagines her own personal melodrama with the assertion that Syria is waiting for her to return one day. The poem opens, "I left Syria many years ago, as a child, / and I don't remember Syria / but Syria remembers me: / I am sure of it." She details the various ways her birth country is waiting for her return: "Syria keeps a small pillow / embroidered with my name / Syria is saving some cherries / in a bowl for me / at the back of the refrigerator." In her vision of this prodigal return, she creates a utopian land:

> I am sure that if I went back to Syria,
> there would be music
> and all the melodrama of a Hindi movie:
> The ground would love me
> The trees would lean toward me like aunts
> The mountains would protect me like cousins
> The ancient churches would kiss my forehead
> . . . .
> Every morning would smell like coffee and cardamom
> Every afternoon would taste like coriander and mint
> Every evening would linger like the music of the oud
> We would all stretch out on the roof under the stars,
> eating nuts and drinking tea in small flowered glasses

Later in the poem, she acknowledges that this vision is utter fantasy, still she insists, "This is my poem and I can do what I want / with the world in it." She explains that she is creating her own soap opera, casting Syria as "a poor woman with a cruel master / who wouldn't let her care for me / as a child deserves to be cared for." Like a child who has been put up for adoption, the ideal dream of the native parent will always exert the strongest pull on her.

In another poem, "The Dream of Return," Kahf imagines returning to Syria at the age of 30. She opens the poem with a reference to the blood in her veins: "It's October and she's turning / thirty, holding out her arm / like a branch, turning the green / leaf over, finding its veins of gold, / its shocking bloodred patterns." In this dream, she conjures her grandparents' home in order to answer questions fundamental to her sense of identity: "What is the riddle of father and mother? / What was the shell of knowledge / that encased her on the day of her birth?" In it, she imagines family vignettes:

> This is the merchant's family
> in the old quarter of the city.

This is the price of oil
we rub on the infant's head and belly.
This is the woolen carpet

silencing the footfall of the mother.
Here are father's small cups
on the beaten copper tray.
. . . .

Smoke that curls from his nostrils
writes stories that will hang
in the air for fifty years.
These are the crossed arms
of mother, her voice

shrilling up the stairwell spiral,
the deep well at the center of the house.

Later in the poem, she revisits the collective memory of her family. She imagines it in terms of opening the door of an old house:

One day a granddaughter turns thirty
In October, like a leaf turning gold,
falling from a tree in the four winds.
She drives into an old, old city.

She puts a key she didn't know she had
into a door and it fits.
. . . .

Like an archaeologist, she finds the remains of her family emotions and stories in this metaphorical house as if they are actual, tangible objects.

She sees the mother's reproaches
lying where they were flung,
hard and small. She sees curlicued
stories hanging in the air like dust.
She lifts up a sheet.

These are the very cups
on the copper tray.
This is the rim marked red

with remembrance, horror, love,
her own blood filling
this deep well

Her own blood comes from this "deep well," meaning that she is a part of this collective family memory. As a writer, it is from this deep reserve of memory and tradition that Kahf mines for her own meaning and identity.

The Terrorist Attacks of September 11, 2001

Another theme in Kahf's collection are the attacks that occurred in the United States on September 11, 2001. In the powerful and stirring poem "We Will Continue Like Twin Towers," Kahf opens with the haunting image of a man and woman who leapt together from the burning towers. Using this image as a point of comparison to the Middle East, she links world events through their simultaneous violence and humanity: "Like the bride and groom of bombed Beirut / who walked across death-filled debris to marry, / even knowing that beneath their feet / everything that kills hope was being unleashed, / they held fast to the handclasp." It is the handclasp, the linking of one person to another, that Kahf wants to emphasize and bring to light. She is speaking to an American audience, presumably, when she writes, "I will continue to invite your children / to play with my children." She then asks the reader, "Will you continue to want your children / to come and go with mine?" The message she is conveying is one of the fragility of life, as well as our mutual dependence on one another as human beings.

We will continue to walk the earth
carrying our small supplies of grace
We will continue to fly even now
that we have been so harshly reminded

of what we can never forget again:
That our lives have always been as fragile,
as dependent on each other, and as beautiful
as the flight of the woman and the man,

twin towers in my sight,
who jumped into the last air hand and hand

The idea of being twinned, of being linked together, is also used in another, shorter poem, "The Fires Have Begun." In it, Kahf employs the symbol of the Twin Towers as being mirrors of the love and hate in all human beings:

There is a World Love Center inside my ribcage.
There is a World Hate Center inside me too.
The fires have begun. The fires have begun,
And I don't know which one
Is going to crumble first.

The haunting image of the two burning towers is used as a rhetorical device to point out the opposing tendencies and influences with which we all struggle.

In another poem dated from 2001, "Learning to Pray All Over," Kahf writes about wanting to add a "spiritual dimension" to her life. Though not a specific reference to September 11, the poem captures the shift in paradigms that occurred for many people at that time.

Soon, like the second half of an eclipse,
The dark will shift. I'll come to know
That all this time I had been living
On a quarter of the light the real sun has.
That thing that trains and forces souls
to pray will move aside. I'll fall down,

as if blind, with my unused eyes. Groping,
I will discover the knobs and knots
In the wall of my own soul. Opening
Its door, I will emerge to fields
Of sorrows and wildflowers. I will find
Rock, stream, tree, wind, road

These, these will become my daily prayers.

Kahf, a practicing Muslim, writes about her religion in this poem in a way that is free from doctrine or ideology. She is interested in finding a direct spiritual experience that is not the "thing that trains and forces souls to pray" but, rather, something that will help her discover her own internal contact with the divine.

CHRONOLOGY

1883
- Kahlil Gibran is born in the town of Bsharri, in Ottoman Syria (present-day northern Lebanon) to a Christian Maronite family.

1895
- The Gibran family sets sail for New York.

1904
- Fred Holland Day hosts Gibran's first exhibition of drawings at his studio in Boston.

1918
- Gibran's *The Madman* is published, his first work in English.

1920
- Along with Lebanese writer Mikhail Naimy, Kahlil Gibran forms the first Arab-American literary society, known as *al-Mahjar*, or the New York Pen League.

1923
- Gibran's *The Prophet* is published.

1925
- Malcolm X is born as Malcolm Little in Omaha, Nebraska.

1928
- Samuel John Hazo is born in Pittsburgh, Pennsylvania, on July 19, to Sam and Lottie (Abdou) Hazo.

1931
- Kahlil Gibran dies in New York City from cirrhosis of the liver and tuberculosis.

1934
- Amiri Baraka is born Everett LeRoi Jones on October 7 in Newark, New Jersey.

1943
- Malcolm X moves to Harlem, New York.

1945
- World War II ends; Egypt, Iraq, Lebanon, Saudi Arabia, Syria, Jordan, and Yemen form the Arab League to coordinate policy between the Arab states.

1946
- Malcolm X is arrested and sentenced to ten years in prison.

1948
- The British Mandate of Palestine is terminated; Israel declares itself an independent nation.
- The Arab-Israeli War begins, the first in a series of wars between the newly declared state of Israel and its Arab neighbors.

1952
- Naomi Shihab Nye is born in St. Louis, Missouri, to a Palestinian father and an American mother.
- Malcolm X is released from prison on parole; he joins the Nation of Islam and changes his surname to X.

1953
- Malcolm X is named assistant minister of the Nation of Islam's Temple Number One in Detroit.

1957
- Mona Simpson is born in Green Bay, Wisconsin, to an American mother and a Syrian father.

1960
- Amiri Baraka goes to Cuba, a visit that begins his transformation into a politically active artist.

1964
- Malcolm X makes a *hajj*, or pilgrimage, to Mecca.
- The Palestine Liberation Organization (PLO) is founded.

- Amiri Baraka's acclaimed, controversial play *Dutchman* premieres and receives an Obie Award.

1965

- Malcolm X is assassinated in New York City on February 21.
- *The Autobiography of Malcolm X* by Alex Haley is published.
- The Black Arts movement is started by Amiri Baraka in Harlem.
- Khaled Hosseini is born in Kabul, Afghanistan.

1966

- Claire Messud is born in Connecticut to a Canadian mother and a French-Algerian father.

1967

- Mohja Kahf is born in Damascus, Syria.

1968

- Amiri Baraka co-edits *Black Fire: An Anthology of Afro-American Writing*, with Larry Neal.

1971

- Mohja Kahf and her family move from Syria to the United States, first settling in Utah.

1973

- Samuel Hazo is named a National Book Award finalist for his book of poetry *Once for the Last Bandit*.

1978

- The Communist Party in Afghanistan seizes power through a bloody coup in April; the Soviets invade Afghanistan in December of that year and remain until 1989.

1979

- Egypt, under President Anwar Sadat, concludes a peace treaty with Israel, ending the prospects of a united Arab military front.

1980

- Khaled Hosseini's family seeks political asylum in the United States and relocates to San Jose, California.

1982

- The Lebanon War breaks out when Israel invades southern Lebanon.

1984

• Amiri Baraka's *The Autobiography of LeRoi Jones/Amiri Baraka* is published.

1986

• Mona Simpson's novel *Anywhere but Here* is published.

1988

• Naomi Shihab Nye receives the Academy of American Poets' Lavan Award, selected by W. S. Merwin.

1990

• The Persian Gulf War begins; U.S. and coalition forces expel Iraqi troops from Kuwait.

1992

• Spike Lee's film *Malcolm X*, based on his autobiography, is released.
• Mona Simpson's second novel, *The Lost Father*, is published.

1993

• Samuel Hazo is appointed the first state poet of the Commonwealth of Pennsylvania by Governor Robert Casey.

1995

• Claire Messud's first novel, *When the World Was Steady*, is published.

1996

• Mona Simpson's *A Regular Guy* is published.

1999

• Claire Messud's novel *The Last Life* is published.

2000

• Mona Simpson's fourth book, a novella titled *Off Keck Road*, is published.

2001

• The World Trade Center in New York City and the Pentagon in Washington, D.C., are attacked by al-Qaeda terrorists on September 11.
• The United States invades Afghanistan in response to the attacks, initiating a conflict there.

2002

• Naomi Shihab Nye's *19 Varieties of Gazelle: Poems of the Middle East* is published.

- Amiri Baraka's appointment as New Jersey's poet laureate is revoked due to a controversial poem he published about the terrorist attacks of September 11, 2001.

2003

- Khaled Hosseini's first novel, *The Kite Runner*, is published.
- Mohja Kahf's first book of poetry, *E-mails from Scheherazad*, is published.
- The United States invades Iraq, which marks the beginning of the Iraq War.

2005

- Naomi Shihab Nye's poetry collection *You and Yours* is published.
- Samuel Hazo's collection of poems titled *A Flight to Elsewhere* is published.

2006

- Khaled Hosseini is named goodwill envoy to the United Nations Refugee Agency.
- Mohja Kahf's novel *The Girl in the Tangerine Scarf* is published.
- Amiri Baraka's short story collection *Tales of the Out & the Gone* is published.
- Claire Messud's *The Emperor's Children* is published.

2007

- Khaled Hosseini's second book, *A Thousand Splendid Suns*, is published.

2008

- Samuel Hazo's *Song of the Horse: A Selection of Poems 1958–2008* is published.

ADDITIONAL READING

Arabian Jazz by Diana Abu-Jaber

This novel, Abu-Jaber's first, focuses on the Ramoud family, the widower Matusseum and his two American-born daughters, Melvina and Jemorah, living in a rundown, less than desirable neighborhood. The women's aunt, scandalized that her adult nieces are still unmarried, sets out to find suitable matches; but her vision of traditional Jordanian marriages does not conform to the hopes and desires of her Westernized nieces. Stuck between two worlds, Melvina and Jemorah strive to balance their American lives with the expectations placed on them by their family and culture.

The Autobiography of LeRoi Jones by Amiri Baraka

Amiri Baraka tells the story of his multifaceted career, in which he has evolved from music critic to literary Beat poet to controversial and incendiary political figure. Starting with his youth in Newark, New Jersey, he traces his early artistic influence from the Greenwich Village of the 1950s to the cultural upheaval of the Black Arts movement in the 1960s, when Baraka moved to Harlem, changed his name, and embraced a religious hybrid of Islamic and traditional African principles. His story concludes in the 1970s, when Baraka turned his back on black nationalism and embraced Marxist Leninism. The autobiography is written in Baraka's unique "word jazz" style.

Crescent by Diana Abu-Jaber

This lyrical novel is set in Los Angeles's Arab-American community and traces the romantic fortunes of its thirty-nine-year-old, half-Arab protagonist, Sirine, a chef in a popular Lebanese restaurant. Centering on Sirine's relationship with the Iraqi academic Hanif, this food-filled novel also explores the various issues underpinning the lives of Arab-American immigrants living in the United States today, as they attempt to forge a new existence and balance expectation and happiness.

The Flag of Childhood: Poems from the Middle East by Naomi Shihab Nye

Naomi Shihab Nye selects 60 poems for this anthology gleaned from the work of Middle Eastern poets, published in response to the terrorist attacks of September 11, 2001. Nye writes in the introduction in response to the notion that "everything has changed," "I would like to think that nothing has changed . . . our need to know one another and to care about other people's lives . . . our ability to grow in our perceptions, to know more than we used to know, to empathize with distant situations and sorrows and joys . . . the power of words to convey truths, across miles and water and time." Poems from Palestine, Israel, Egypt, Iraq, and elsewhere give a view into the human connections of family and friends, as well as providing a vivid and indelible sense of place.

The Girl in the Tangerine Scarf by Mohja Kahf

This novel, Kahf's first, follows the story of Syrian immigrant Khadra Shamy, spanning from childhood to adulthood. Khadra grows up in a devout, tightly knit Muslim family in 1970s Indiana. Along with her brother, Eyad, and her African-American friends, Hakim and Hanifa, she grows up navigating the uncomfortable space that exists between her culture and the mainstream American experience. The novel shifts perspective from Khadra's return to Indiana as an adult who has lost her youthful idealism to the events that caused her to escape years before.

The Last Life by Claire Messud

Messud's second novel follows three generations of the LaBasse family and is set in colonial Algeria, the south of France, and New England. Told from the first-person perspective of adolescent Sagesse LaBasse, the novel traces her family's emigration from Algiers during the political turmoil of the 1950s. They build a new life in the south of France running a successful hotel. Their world is shattered, however, by a single event, and, in the process, family secrets emerge.

The Lost Father by Mona Simpson

The heroine from Simpson's novel *Anywhere but Here* returns to search for her missing father in the story of an idealized father-daughter relationship. Now a woman of twenty-eight and finally on her own in medical school, Ann August—who has changed her name to Mayan—becomes obsessed with the father she never knew. She hires detectives to dredge up the past, loses her savings, and ruins her fledgling career over the course of an extensive search spanning two continents.

Malcolm X Speaks: Selected Speeches and Statements edited by George Breitman

This volume collects the major speeches made by Malcolm X during the last volatile eight months of his life, including his letters from his pilgrimage abroad. In this short period of time, his vision for abolishing racial inequality in the United States underwent a major transformation. In this period, he breaks from the Nation of Islam and moves away from the black militarism that dominated his early thinking, expanding his philosophy of the nature of race in the United States.

A Thousand Splendid Suns by Khaled Hosseini

Hosseini's second novel focuses on the lives of two Afghan women—Mariam and Laila. Though born a generation apart, both women witness the destruction of their homes and families in war-torn Kabul over the course of thirty years, spanning from the 1960s to 2003. Their lives are brought together through a series of tragic events, in which the personal and the political are woven into each other, revealing how recent historical events impact the lives of individuals—particularly the fragile and precarious lives of Afghan girls and women.

BIBLIOGRAPHY

Primary Texts

The Autobiography of Malcolm X as Told to Alex Haley. New York: Ballantine Books, 1987. Print.

Baraka, Imamu Amiri. *Tales of the Out & the Gone*. New York: Akashic Books, 2006. Print.

Baraka, Imamu Amiri, and William J. Harris, *The LeRoi Jones/Amiri Baraka Reader*. New York: Thunder's Mouth Press, 1991. Print.

Gibran, Kahlil. *The Prophet*. New York: Knopf, 2006. Print.

Hazo, Samuel. *Song of the Horse: A Selection of Poems 1958–2008*. Pittsburgh: Autumn House, 2008. Print.

Hosseini, Khaled. *The Kite Runner*. New York: Riverhead Books, 2003. Print.

Kahf, Mohja. *E-mails from Scheherazad*. Gainesville: University of Florida, 2003. Print.

Messud, Claire. *The Emperor's Children*. New York: Vintage Books, 2007. Print.

Shihab Nye, Naomi. *19 Varieties of Gazelle: Poems of the Middle East*. New York: Harper Collins, 2002. Print.

Simpson, Mona. *Anywhere but Here*. New York: Vintage, 1992. Print.

Secondary Texts

Abdelrazek, Amal Talaat. *Contemporary Arab American Women Writers: Hyphenated Identities and Border Crossings*. New York: Cambria, 2008. Print.

Akash, Munir and Khaled Mattawa, eds. *Post-Gibran Anthology of New Arab American Writing*. W. Bethesda, Md.: Kitab, Inc., 1999. Print.

Baraka, Imamu Amiri and Charlie Reilly, *Conversations with Amiri Baraka*. Jackson: University Press of Mississippi, 1994. Print.

Benston, Kimberly W., *Imamu Amiri Baraka (Leroi Jones): A Collection of Critical Essays*. Englewood Cliffs, N.J.: Prentice-Hall, 1978. Print.

Bushrui, Suheil B. *Kahlil Gibran: Man and Poet, A New Biography*. Oxford, England: Oneworld, 1999. Print.

Hudson, Theodore R., *From LeRoi Jones to Amiri Baraka: The Literary Works*. Durham, N.C.: Duke University Press, 1973. Print.

Kadi, Joanna, ed. *Food for Our Grandmothers: Writings by Arab-American and Arab-Canadian Feminists*. Cambridge, Mass.: South End Press, 1994. Print.

Kahf, Mohja, *Western Representations of the Muslim Woman: From Termagant to Odalisque*. Austin: University of Texas Press, 1999. Print.

Muaddi Darraj, Susan, ed. *Scheherazade's Legacy: Arab and Arab-American Women on Writing*. Westport, Conn.: Praeger, 2004. Print.

Salaita, Steven George. *Arab American Literary Fictions, Cultures, and Politics*. New York: Palgrave Macmillan, 2007. Print.

Waterfield, Robin. *Prophet: The Life and Times of Kahlil*. New York: Penguin Putnam, 1998. Print.

Web Sites

Amiri Baraka's official Web site
http://www.amiribaraka.com/

Arab American Institute
http://www.aaiusa.org/

Claire Messud book review in the *New York Times*
http://www.nytimes.com/2006/08/27/books/review/ORourke.html

Kahlil Gibran at the Cornell Library site
http://www.library.cornell.edu/colldev/mideast/gibrn.htm

Khaled Hosseini's official Web site
http://www.khaledhosseini.com/

Mohja Kahf article in the *New York Times*
http://www.nytimes.com/2007/05/12/books/12veil.html

Naomi Shihab Nye at Poets.org
http://www.poets.org/poet.php/prmPID/174

Naomi Shihab Nye interview with Bill Moyers
http://www.pbs.org/now/transcript/transcript_nye.html

INDEX

PICTURE CREDITS

ABOUT THE AUTHOR

REBECCA LAYTON is an artist and writer living in Austin, Texas. She studied literature at Barnard College and fine art at Hunter College. When not writing or making art, she teaches a summer art history course in Barcelona, Spain. She is the illustrator of the biography *Life List: A Woman's Quest for the World's Most Amazing Birds* (2009).